Issues in Education

GENERAL EDITOR: PHILIP HILLS

In-Service Education and Training

Other Books in This Series

Gordon Batho: *Political Issues in Education*
David Bosworth: *Open Learning*
Paul Fisher: *Education 2000*
Roy Todd: *Education in a Multicultural Society*

Michael Williams

In-Service Education and Training
Policy and Practice

CASSELL

Cassell Educational Limited
Villiers House
41/47 Strand
London WC2N 5JE

First published 1991

British Library Cataloguing in Publication Data
Williams, Michael
  In-service education and training: policy and practice. –
  (Issues in education).
  1. England. Schools. Teachers. In-service training – Case
  studies
  I. Title II. Series
  371.1460942

  ISBN 0-304-32290-3
  ISBN 0-304-31958-9 pbk

Typeset by Litho Link Ltd, Welshpool, Powys, Wales

Printed in Great Britain by Biddles Ltd, Guildford and King's
Lynn

Contents

Foreword: The purpose of this series

The educational scene is changing rapidly. This change is being caused by a complexity of factors which includes a re-examination of present educational provision against a background of changing social and economic policies, the 1988 Education Reform Act, new forms of testing and assessment, a National Curriculum, and local management of schools with more participation by parents.

As the educational process is concerned with every aspect of our lives and our society both now and for the future, it is of vital importance that all teachers, teachers in training, administrators and educational policy-makers should be aware and informed on current issues in education.

This series of books is thus designed to inform on current issues, look at emerging ones, and to give an authoritative overview which will be of immense help to all those involved in the education process.

Philip Hills
Cambridge

Acknowledgements

This book could not have been written without the experience gained in INSET work initially at Jordanhill College of Education in Glasgow in the 1960s and then in the Department of Education at the University of Manchester. As Director of the Centre for INSET at the University of Manchester I was fortunate to work closely with a large number of LEAs in the north-west of England, particularly at the time of TRIST and the first years of the LEA Training Grants Scheme. INSET evaluation studies which I conducted and supervised for some of these LEAs were challenging and educative. They yielded a number of reports on which I have drawn in this book. My debt to those evaluators who were seconded to study with me in Manchester will be obvious to them in the following pages. I have been privileged to work alongside John England, Barbara Fonseca and Philip Mather on interesting and productive projects.

It is customary to render reference to LEAs and schools anonymous in much published writing and I have adhered to that convention. Similarly, I have sought to avoid reference by name to those chief advisers and INSET advisers in the ten LEAs that constituted the former Greater Manchester, from whom I learned so much before I moved to my current post in Wales. In the field of INSET in England the north-western LEAs were at the cutting edge in the early 1980s. The camaraderie and professional relationships established across LEA boundaries and between LEAs and INSET providers in institutions of higher education were enormous assets which facilitated the development of a rich and flexible set of INSET arrangements.

It is always difficult to name individuals since there is the danger that someone important will be inadvertently overlooked. However, I would like to acknowledge the considerable guidance I have received in seeking to understand the intricacies of INSET provision from my LEA colleagues: Trevor Smalley (Bury and 'Greater Manchester'), Bill Dempsey and Norman Barton (Oldham), Alan Pemberton and Ann Hillerton (Salford), Tony Lavin (Bolton), Roy Bacon (Manchester), Bill Greenwood (Wigan), Tony Bedford (Trafford), Edward Blundell (Stockport), Cliff Bentley and Don Edge (Rochdale). They are all pioneers in the development of INSET in the North-West and have devoted considerable time and energy to seeking to establish the best forms of INSET for the teachers in their areas. Much of that time was spent in collaborative and constructive discussions and planning meetings, in some of which I was fortunate to be a participant.

Away from the British scene, I have benefited from the collaborative work in which I have been engaged with overseas friends and colleagues. In particular, I was introduced to continental European INSET experience by Professor Roland Hahn (Stuttgart), Professor Hartwig Haubrich (Freiburg), Drs Henk Meijer (Utrecht), Professor Ove Biilmann and Tonny Hubbe (Copenhagen). With Ove Biilmann and Dr Rod Gerber (Brisbane) it has been my good fortune to work on an international INSET project which was published by the Education Commission of the International Geographical Union and from which new work is currently being developed.

I am grateful to the following for permission to use material published elsewhere: the Controller of Her Majesty's Stationery Office (extracts on pp. 3, 4, 8, 11, 13, 14, 21–2, 23–4, 26, 27, 43, 78, 79); the Training Agency (extracts on pp. 17, 18, 20, 41–2, 44–8, 162, 163, 164–5); John Wiley & Sons Ltd (pp. 1, 7); Studies in Education Ltd (p. 142); and Dr Colin Robson (pp. 115–16, 166–7).

Introduction

In a relatively short period of time a remarkable change has occurred in the attention paid to the in-service education and training of teachers (INSET) in England and Wales. This largely reflects the speed of change in school organization, management and curricula. The shift from an educational system based upon pupil selection at 11+ to a comprehensive system of secondary schooling was an important stimulus to enhancing the professional competence of schoolteachers in primary and secondary schools. The key issues were brought to the fore during the course of the Great Debate that was launched in 1976 and these were reinforced by the Technical and Vocational Education Initiative (TVEI) after 1983, the TVEI related INSET programme (TRIST), the reorganization of public examinations for pupils aged 16 and over, and the proposals for a National Curriculum encompassed in the Education Reform Act of 1988. These changes were fundamental and far-reaching, affecting the daily work of all teachers of pupils in the compulsory years of schooling. Not all teachers were affected equally or simultaneously. What has emerged is a complicated map of INSET provision in which individual schools, clusters of schools, local education authorities, a number of independent agencies, teacher training institutions and government departments are located. All of these are in a dynamic state and any attempt to describe accurately the map at any particular moment must inevitably run the risk of soon being out-dated and inaccurate. One has only to observe the proposals made at the end of the 1980s for the initial training of teachers to appreciate how major structural changes may be introduced one after another in a very short period of time. Similarly, major changes may be introduced in INSET at local and national levels.

This book focuses on the principles and practice of INSET in the context of contemporary changes in England and Wales. It is written largely from the perspective of an INSET provider and draws heavily upon the experience of the writer in organizing, participating in, and evaluating a variety of INSET activities. Where appropriate, information from overseas is included.

In terms of attention paid by scholars and researchers, INSET is a Cinderella topic. It has been largely unresearched, being more the subject for recommendation and pragmatic action than the target for incremental and large-scale, heavily funded studies. Throughout the following chapters an attempt will be made to blend the findings that are available from academic studies with evidence from a variety of sources. The style of presentation has been chosen to suit the intended readership. It is hoped that the contents will be of interest to senior staff in primary and secondary schools, especially those who have a specific responsibility for INSET matters, and to INSET providers and organizers, including local education authority (LEA) staff and INSET specialists in institutions of higher education.

The pattern 'where are we now, where are we going, how are we going to get there?' provides the framework for what follows. It is important for all participants in INSET, clients, planners, managers and providers, to have a clear understanding of context. This context has a number of dimensions, including historical, political, financial, structural, managerial and professional aspects. These are complex and difficult to disentangle. In seeking to offer an analytical perspective there is a danger that issues may appear over-simplified and distorted. Readers who are seeking immediate answers to day-to-day problems are counselled to be patient if the amount of attention paid to context appears to be excessive. We are all aware of the difficulties encountered in seeking to translate someone else's experience into our own situation. Professional behaviour is circumscribed by local, regional and national contexts. Variations in behaviour are the most striking characteristic of the educational scene. An attempt has been made to offer generalizations in both principles and practice and a deliberate effort has been made to offer information and guidance that ought to assist in the development of good practice.

Running through the text is the argument that as much attention should be paid to the curriculum and organization of INSET as is currently being paid to the school curriculum and to the curriculum of pre-service teacher education in England and Wales. Arguments about how to ensure progression, differentiation, balance, breadth, coherence and relevance are as valid to the continuing professional development of teachers as they are to other sectors of education. Without this sustained developmental professional view the arrangements made for INSET will always appear to be *ad hoc* and reactive to the whims of the policy-makers, and the needs of teachers for continuing professional development will be relatively neglected.

The sequence of chapters in this book is predictable. It begins with a discussion of the principal changes that have taken place in INSET in the years following the Second World War. The emphasis is largely upon the past 15 years, with most attention given to offering an explanation of current practice. In this historical context we can trace the steps towards a planned system in which schools, LEAs, providers and central government agencies interlock within particular political and financial frameworks.

In Chapter 2 I concentrate upon the role of LEAs, with the bulk of the chapter being made up of case-studies of selected LEAs. These illustrate the planning structures they have established to provide INSET within and between their boundaries.

This is followed in Chapter 3 with a consideration of the planning arrangements for INSET within schools. As in LEAs, we have witnessed in recent years the emergence of a cadre of professionals who have been given specific responsibilities for staff development and INSET in schools. The distinction between staff development and INSET is explored and an attempt is made to locate INSET within the overall management concerns of schools.

At the heart of INSET planning is the identification of training needs of individual teachers, functional groups in schools and whole school staffs. A needs-based model of INSET planning and provision has been advocated for many years but it is only in recent years that serious steps have been taken to put proposals into practice. This translation from principles to practice is the subject of Chapter 4.

Once needs have been identified, the next step is to design and implement appropriate INSET activities. Conventionally, INSET has been provided largely through the organization of courses. Such courses have frequently been *ad hoc*, organized by agencies at a distance from schools and designed to capture a general audience. They have lacked thorough preparation of the participants and thorough follow-up once the course has terminated. In recent years there have been substantial moves away from these conventions and these changes are traced in Chapter 5. Courses have changed in their design and delivery. In particular, institutions of higher education have experimented with new ways of providing award-bearing INSET activities, which may or may not include conventional courses, and these are discussed in this chapter.

Alternatives to conventional courses are the subject for Chapter 6. There are three focal points: curriculum development projects that implicitly or explicitly incorporate INSET programmes; consultancy models; and distance learning models.

In Chapter 7 the focus is upon procedures for monitoring and evaluating INSET. As activity in INSET has increased and as more money has been allocated for INSET developments the demand by those who hold the purse strings for more attention to be paid to monitoring and evaluation has also been heard more clearly. In a climate of delegated budgets and financial austerity within the education system it is important for all those persons and agencies involved in INSET to consider the importance of value for money. Much lip-service is paid to monitoring and evaluation and in this chapter an attempt is made to clarify some of the difficulties and indicate some of the solutions.

Finally, in Chapter 8, a tentative attempt is made to predict the future of INSET. It is possible to extrapolate from current practices those trends that give some insight to the future. However, educational progress and change are always unpredictable and much of what is written in this final chapter is highly speculative.

1 INSET: establishing the patterns

Background to contemporary developments

Given that pre-service teacher education was not regarded by central government as a necessity for all schoolteachers in state secondary schools until 1973, it is not surprising that in-service teacher education has not been high on the educational agenda. In the absence of central government concern, other agencies fulfilled the role of up-dating teachers' professional knowledge and skills. Insufficient credit has been given to the contributions made by specialist voluntary associations of teachers and other agencies, which provided an array of publications, conferences and courses for teachers. This is not to say that INSET was totally ignored by central and local government bodies, since a number of official reports on various aspects of education had highlighted its importance.

It was the McNair Commission Report of 1944 (Board of Education) that drew attention to the inadequacies of the arrangements for pre-service teacher education in England and Wales. As Turner (1973, p. 150) commented:

> Two distinguishing marks of the training colleges at the time of the McNair Report were their poverty and their small size. 'What is chiefly wrong with the majority of the training colleges', said the Report, 'is their poverty and all that flows from it'. Of the eighty-three training colleges in 1938, sixty-four had fewer than 150 students and twenty-eight of those had fewer than a hundred. The paragraphs on conditions in the colleges made depressing reading. In fifty per cent of the colleges it was judged that laboratories, studios, workshops and gymnasia were considered inadequate.

1

Such a foundation was hardly appropriate for establishing an adequate system for the continuing professional development of teachers in post-war England and Wales. Not that a system, if it meant centralized direction and control, was a desirable target in the eyes of some of the McNair Commission members. Notice the assertion made by some of its members: 'We reject, however, anything approaching permanent central control over the training of teachers. Centralisation of power and authority has potential dangers in every sphere of education and nowhere are those dangers so great and subtle as in the training of teachers' (Board of Education 1944a, pp. 49–50). In seeking to understand how the contemporary pattern has come about, it is necessary to consider the concepts of power and authority with reference to the interaction between individual teachers, the schools in which they work, the local education authorities in which they are employed and the Department of Education and Science.

It is interesting to notice the language employed in the McNair Report for INSET. Their chosen term is 'refresher courses for serving teachers'. Regarding such courses, there is a recommendation in the Report that 'the Joint Board should be made responsible for organising the provision of Refresher and other Courses for serving teachers given either on university premises or on the premises of training colleges or on both, and during either term or vacations . . . The courses should be both professional and upon specific subjects on which the teachers wish to refresh or add to their knowledge . . . We think it probable that the Joint Board will play an important part both in making the necessary arrangements for teachers to be allowed sabbatical terms and in helping them to make the best use of them' (Board of Education 1944a, p. 58).

In the immediate post-war years the emergency training of new cohorts of teachers, many of them recently returned from war service, was the top priority. Circular 1652 had been produced by the Board of Education, the predecessor of the Department of Education and Science, on 15 May 1944. The circular specified the aims of the post-war scheme:

We do not regard the students to be trained under the Emergency Scheme as mere stop-gaps who are to be rushed into the schools to tide over the immediate crisis. If the scheme is justified at all, they must, like other students in training, be regarded as *potential* teachers in the fullest sense, who are, through the training course, to be started along the path of which, partly through subsequent training of various kinds, they may, when they receive their full recognition, take their place as equals beside teachers who have entered the profession through other and more usual channels. (Board of Education 1944b)

By 1950, when the emergency scheme terminated, some 27,000 students had passed through the 55 specially created Emergency Training Colleges. This was the first cycle of post-war reform of teacher education and was to be followed in the ensuing period by a number of major reforms and reorganizations. Not surprisingly, INSET took a back seat, a seat it occupied until it was brought to the fore in the proposals of the James Report in 1972.

The period from 1950 to 1970 was one of educational expansion. Local education authorities sought to establish new urban and rural services for expanding communities. Rehousing, evidenced most strikingly in suburban public and private housing estates and the designation and construction of new towns, was accompanied by the building of new primary and secondary schools. Similar expansion was witnessed in higher education with the expansion of universities in size and numbers, the advent of polytechnics and the growth in teacher training institutions. Not only were institutions changing in size, they were also being reformed. The changes were heralded and recorded in a series of major educational reports commissioned by central government. With regard to schools, the most important of these were the reports of the Central Advisory Council for Education, which included comprehensive and authoritative studies of early leaving (1954, Chair Sir Samuel Gurney-Dixon), 15–18 (1959, Chair Sir Geoffrey Crowther), technical education in Wales (1961, Chair Mr A. B. Oldfield Davies), pupils of less than average ability (1963, Chair Mr John Newsom), and children and their primary schools in England

(1967, Chair Lady Plowden) and Wales (1968, Chair Professor Charles Gittins).

The expansion of secondary education had implications both for the availability of places in higher education and for the content of courses at that level. The Report of the Committee on Higher Education (the Robbins Report), published in 1963, contained a broad overview of the current position and future possibilities of higher education. It built on the White Paper on Technical Education (1956), which heralded the creation of colleges of advanced technology that later gained university charters.

For the teacher training colleges, which had concentrated on preparing teachers to work primarily in primary schools via three-year courses leading to a certificate, the Robbins Report proposed some substantial changes:

> We recommend a radical change. The status of the colleges would best be assured and the problem of degrees satisfactorily solved by a closer association with the universities. Our recommendation is that, as a development from the Institutes of Education in which the colleges are at present associated with the universities, there should be set up University Schools of Education under whose auspices degrees would be available to suitable college students ... Training Colleges, which should be renamed Colleges of Education, would be given independent governing bodies; they would become members of the Schools of Education and would receive finance from them.

In addition to recommending closer affiliation to universities, a change of name and greater autonomy, the Report also recommended the introduction of a four-year degree programme for intending teachers, which would include academic study and professional preparation. The implementation of these recommendations saw the expansion of the colleges as they set about developing new BEd degrees. Close affiliation with the universities was not achieved by all the colleges since some of them preferred to have their awards validated by the Council for National Academic Awards (CNAA), a new body that had been recommended by the Robbins Report and that was established in February 1964.

Following the publication of the Robbins Report there was a struggle between various interested parties over the control of the colleges of education. This struggle has been thoroughly analysed by Paul Sharp (1987) in his detailed study of the creation of the local authority sector of higher education, which describes the interaction between the various pressure groups with vested interests in teacher education. This interaction was played against a backcloth of institutional expansion in the 1960s and sharp contraction and rationalization in the 1970s and 1980s. The comment of Stuart Maclure, made in a lecture given at the 1983 annual conference of the Universities Council for the Education of Teachers (UCET), is not surprising:

> In recent years it has been an article of faith for the Powers that Be that some sort of almighty upheaval in teacher education is needed every year or two in case everybody goes to sleep or worse still, gets on quietly with his or her own job. It reminds you of one of those nightmare hospitals where they insist on waking patients up in the middle of the night to check they have taken their sleeping pills.

Such fluctuations in policy were a product of the dynamic national economic context coincidental with the reform of school education. Moves towards comprehensive secondary education, with the consequent loss of the 11+ examination in primary schools, witnessed a different kind of struggle. Here the struggle was for the school curriculum. Did comprehensive education mean a reformulation of whole school curricular aims and specialist subject transformations, the modification of courses and their content, and the revision of modes of assessment? If such major reforms were necessary, how were these to be brought about and by whom? The comprehensivization of secondary schools and the raising of the school leaving age from 15 to 16 years provided the impetus for the establishment of the Schools Council for Curriculum and Examinations in 1964.

The Schools Council strengthened the alliance between teachers and their employers, i.e. the local education authorities, and these were the two dominant partners in the triangular relationship that was at the heart of its organization. The third partner was the DES, which in the mid-1960s had a low profile with regard to the school curriculum. Significantly absent from the management of the Schools Council were the universities and other institutions of higher education. However, the principal activities generated by the Schools Council were curriculum development projects, the majority of which were based in universities or colleges of education. These projects devised a number of different strategies for gathering evidence of good practice and promoting changes in aims and objectives, content, teaching and learning strategies and modes of assessment. The key to the success of the projects lay in their ability to disseminate their findings to teachers. Publications, conferences and courses proliferated, although it was the establishment of teachers' centres by LEAs that was seen as the most appropriate way forward.

Teachers' centres were, and continue to be, an expression of the LEAs' concern for the professional development of their teachers. They have varied markedly from one LEA to another. Some are located in purpose-built buildings, others are located within schools or colleges of education. Some have specialized in particular sectors of schooling or particular areas of the curriculum, others are more broadly based. Some employ large staffs, others have a part-time warden supported by a part-time secretary. They have varied in their functions and in their levels of success. Important to all of them has been attracting teachers from their catchment areas to attend workshops, conferences and courses, arranged usually in out-of-school hours. Central to their concern in the 1960s and 1970s was participation in, and the dissemination of the products of, Schools Council curriculum development projects.

Alan Rudd, Director of the North West Regional Curriculum Development Project in 1972, was well placed to reflect on the emergence of teachers' centres. He posed the question, 'Why should teachers take their professional concerns to local teachers' centres?'

The academic answer usually given is that such centres provide like-minded teachers with a local and relatively unstructured setting within which to discuss professional matters, often as a preliminary to proposing innovation within their own school setting. Yet five years later it has to be confessed that most such centres are still bedevilled by the problem of how to entice teachers into the centres for sustained bouts of professional work. Short in-service courses, exhibitions of teaching materials or of pupils' work, a reference library/resource centre, a workshop for making needed apparatus – all such are valuable services for a teachers' centre to offer. It has been our experience, however, that creative work in curriculum development provides much the strongest stimulus for schools' commitment to the work of teachers' centres. (pp. 322–3).

By 1977 there were some 544 teachers' centres in England and Wales and their work has been reviewed and evaluated by several authors, including Adams (1975), Brugelmann (1976), Redknap (1977), Thornbury (1973) and Weindling *et al.* (1983). There is general acknowledgement of the importance of the Schools Council stimulating their establishment, especially in Working Paper no. 10:

... the motive power should come primarily from local groups of teachers accessible to one another; [and] there should be effective and close collaboration between teachers and all those who are able to offer close collaboration ... that is, the support services of Advisers, Inspectorate and institutions of initial training. (Schools Council 1967)

In this brief extract are contained some of the key constituents of INSET before the publication of the James Report in 1972. There is the element of partnership between teachers and outside school support agencies and, associated with this, the concept of pluralism in control and delivery of INSET. Furthermore, there is the important element of teacher professionalism and the gains to be obtained from collaboration between local groups of teachers. It was in the development of teachers' centres that we can see the origins of the movement towards school-based and school-focused INSET, which we shall return to later. It is sufficient to emphasize at this point that the teachers' centres, although reduced in number, have survived even though the Schools Council was terminated in 1984.

The publication of the James Report, *Teacher Education and Training* (Committee of Inquiry 1972), drew public attention to the need for greater attention to be paid to INSET. At the centre of its recommendations were reform of initial teacher training and close interaction between initial and in-service training. To achieve this a model incorporating three cycles of teacher education and training was promulgated: the first, personal education; the second, pre-service training and induction; and the third, in-service education and training.

The authors of the James Report asserted that much of their argument depended on their proposals for the third cycle. In the introduction to the Report (para. 1.9) it is stated that:

> A large expansion of third cycle provision to give every teacher an entitlement to regular inservice education and training, is an essential precondition of a more realistic and rational approach to initial training in the second cycle . . . Most important of all, it is in the third cycle that the education and training of teachers can be, and should be at its best. It is here that both the quality of our education and the standards of the profession can be most speedily, powerfully and economically improved. (Committee of Inquiry 1972)

Notice the introduction of the word *entitlement* in this quotation, a word that was to take on a special meaning later in the Report (para. 2.22), where it is recommended that:

> As soon as better staffing and the expansion of full-time courses allow, all teachers should be entitled to release with pay for a minimum of one school term or the equivalent (a period of, say, 12 weeks) in a specified number of years. The immediate aim should be to secure teachers' entitlement to a minimum of one term or the equivalent in every seven years, but this should be regarded as only an interim target. As soon as possible, the level of entitlement should be raised to one term in five years.

Central to the Report was the concept of progression in teacher education and training. The transition from personal education leading to a Diploma of Higher Education at the end of the first cycle, through a bachelor's degree and induction into school in the second cycle and on into continuing INSET in the third cycle was seen as the structured route to teacher professionalism. Essential to the infrastructure were more independent training institutions, teachers' centres and professional tutors occupying senior positions in schools. The publication of the Report was followed in the same year by the White Paper, *Education: A Framework for Expansion* (DES/ Welsh Office 1972), which outlined the future pattern of non-university higher education and proposed changes in teacher education in line with the James Report recommendations. Any prospects for expansion were soon dashed as the sharp economic depression brought on by the 1973 oil crisis resulted in financial cuts in public spending and the contraction of teacher training targets. The falling school rolls heralded by the 1971 Census figures were to reinforce the necessity for contraction.

The reform of local government in 1974 saw a reduction in the number of local education authorities, the designation of a number of metropolitan counties, which were short-lived, and the establishment of new teacher support structures. A feature of many LEAs was the appointment of teams of advisers who had INSET as a principal function in their multi-dimensional roles. In response to the needs of schools, increasing attention was paid by LEAs to INSET for school management, the introduction of new technology and multi-cultural education. The publication of the Bullock Report in 1975 and the Cockcroft Report in 1981 focused the eyes of teachers on key subjects and the Warnock Report in 1978 did the same for the education of pupils with special needs.

A growing awareness that all was not well in primary and secondary schools prompted the speech by Prime Minister James Callaghan at Ruskin College in 1976. This marked the beginning of an intense public debate about school organization and school curriculum which reached its head more than ten years later with the passing of the Education Reform Act of 1988. From 1976, schools became familiar with a constant flow

9

of publications, emanating principally from Her Majesty's Inspectorate (HMI) and the Department of Education and Science (DES) but including important and influential documents from subject associations, teachers' unions, examination boards, the Schools Council and an array of community pressure groups. This is not the place to review the 'Great Debate' in any detail. Suffice it to say that by 1981 schools were required to prepare curriculum plans and LEAs were required to submit LEA curriculum plans to the DES. The importance of providing the appropriate INSET to ensure that the plans could be implemented was the spur to the developments that took place in INSET in the years following 1985.

A suitable framework for establishing INSET arrangements in LEAs and schools was provided in a short but punchy document produced by a subcommittee of the Advisory Committee on the Supply and Training of Teachers (1978). Entitled *Making INSET Work*, it was distributed to every school in England and Wales. It remains one of the most useful short guides to good INSET practice.

The subcommittee suggested that in 1978 INSET was 'at a take-off point in this country' and went on to assert that 'if it is to achieve its full potential then every teacher in every school needs to be involved in an on-going discussion about it' (p. 16). The brief booklet was designed to stimulate discussion among teachers within schools and readers were encouraged to send in their comments and suggestions to the subcommittee. Four practical steps were proposed to enable a school to plan its own INSET programme:

1. Identify the main needs.
2. Decide on and implement the general programme.
3. Evaluate the effectiveness of this general programme.
4. Follow up the ideas gained.

These steps were envisaged as being overlapping rather than sequential. The identification of needs was perceived as a dynamic process since identified needs would have to be reconsidered in the light of changing circumstances. Consultation between teachers was advocated, as needs were considered at three levels: the individual teacher, functional groups within a school, and the school as a whole. It was recognized that a distinction could be made between 'those problems occurring in the teacher's everyday classroom and school work', which 'generated needs of a concrete and immediate kind', and the results of teachers taking stock of their careers and deciding what form of INSET, an advanced course involving secondment, for example, would best help them to develop further.

With needs identified, the next step was to decide which needs should be given priority in any term or year. The breadth of provision was referred to in a succinct and comprehensive paragraph (pp. 6–7):

> Before any programme of activity can be planned or requested the staff need information about the range of providing agencies available. Although universities, teachers' centres, colleges and advisers will usually be well known, it is easy to forget that other agencies, for instance reading centres, radio and television, may have something valuable to offer: a place for teachers from several schools to hold a joint conference; reprographic equipment and technical expertise to assist a group making reading games for older infants; a large collection of children's literature and someone who knows what is available; an Open University series which could be used in a staff discussion group. Perhaps most important of all, are not teachers in the same and other schools themselves valuable 'providing agencies'?

Turning to evaluating the programme, the authors of the booklet acknowledged that this is an important and difficult task. They offered a list of questions: Who wants to know and why? Who will carry out the evaluation? What will be evaluated? How will the information be collected? Are the proposed evaluation methods feasible? What procedures, if any, will govern the collection and release of information about the activities and views of those involved? What back-up resources are necessary for the efficient conduct of the evaluation? How can you feed your views back to the organizers so they can make any necessary improvements?

Attention is given to ways of following up ideas gained in attending an INSET activity. Four key questions are posed: 'What procedures are necessary to ensure that the school is made aware of the results of INSET undertaken by you and your colleagues? How can serious consideration be given to changes in your school when an INSET activity is ended? Are there adequate resources, e.g. staff and time, to put the good ideas into practice? If you came back from a course with much wider professional horizons, what kind of re-orientation would you like?'

Finally, consideration was given to the management of INSET in individual schools. Planning and co-ordination were seen as the responsibility of an individual at senior level in a school and the designation of persons as professional tutors was seen as the way forward.

This document paved the way for what followed in the next decade. The stages highlighted in its few pages were to be re-emphasized in DES proposals for INSET planning. They were extended and enhanced in the paper produced by the Advisory Committee on the Supply and Education of Teachers (ACSET) in 1984 and they found further support in the TVEI related INSET (TRIST) scheme of 1985.

The ACSET Report 1984

In March 1983 the Government published the White Paper, *Teaching Quality*, in which it was asserted that:

> In-service training has an important part to play in the career development of teachers. In the Government's view all teachers need from time to time to avail themselves of in-service training. There should also be a closer and clearer relationship between training (including in-service training), experience and qualifications on the one hand and deployment – including promotion – on the other. (DES/Welsh Office 1983, para. 91)

This needs to be read in the context of the changing pattern of teacher employment, which had been discussed earlier in the

White Paper. It was predicted that there would be 'an increase in demand for newly trained primary teachers during the middle and late 1980s, and that during the same period there will be a substantial decline in demand for newly trained secondary teachers, followed by some early recovery in the early 90s' (para. 4). It was this prediction that led ACSET to write (1984):

> It follows that the quality of education will depend, to very large measure, on the quality of teachers already in schools. We are convinced that the development and maintenance of a dynamic, highly motivated and skilled teaching force is directly dependent on recognition of the needs of teachers already in service for further training and professional development and the provision of opportunities to meet those needs.

The ACSET report stated that the case for INSET rested on the needs of the education service, of individual schools and of teachers themselves. The authors reviewed the climate of change in teaching, which included the reform of curricula and examinations, the requirement for new teaching skills resulting from the introduction of microcomputers, the development of pupils' records of achievement and the role of teachers in contributing to the initial training of teachers. Teachers were also expected to understand and relate to the views of parents, governors and representatives of the working world and the wider community. Further, they were expected to be aware of the diversity – in ability, behaviour, social background and ethnic and cultural origins – of their pupils. For senior staff in schools there was a need for improved management training. INSET also had a crucial role in facilitating the redeployment of teachers between schools and between phases. In a context of falling school rolls and a reduction in teachers' promotion prospects, INSET had 'an important role to play in helping teachers to strengthen their sense of purpose and morale' (para. 10).

Close account was taken of the changing nature of schools, the context in which they were expected to function, and the teachers' personal and professional development. 'INSET is likely to be the most effective way of strengthening their confidence and enabling them to re-invigorate their thinking and their approach ... Opportunities to undertake curriculum development and to up-date subject knowledge are needed by all teachers as a normal part of their professional development' (paras 12 and 13). The case was concluded with the rallying cry, 'We consider that the education service owes teachers improved opportunities to enhance their professional development.'

There followed a brief account of INSET provision in which the variety of possibilities was highlighted and the importance of identifying teachers' needs was emphasized. They reported the difficulties of determining the costs of INSET and how these costs were met, and pointed to the variations in funding arrangements for different types of provision, in particular the funding arrangements for long and short INSET courses in institutions of higher education.

One of the strongest statements in the report read: 'The ultimate goal of in-service training is the improvement of pupils' learning, through improvements in school and teacher performance' (para. 36). This statement introduced a discussion of the conditions for the effectiveness of INSET, which focused on nine items (para. 38):

(i)   Identification by teachers of their training needs in relation to the objectives of the school and the LEA and their own professional development;

(ii) support of Governors, the head teacher and senior staff and local authority advisers and involvement of the whole staff;

(iii) a coherent LEA policy (which should include helping schools and colleges also to develop coherent INSET policies);

(iv) precise 'targeting' of provision;

(v)   choice of the appropriate form of INSET whether individual to the teacher, school-based or externally-based;

(vi) choice of appropriate length of course and mode of activity;

(vii) relevance to the teachers' need and focused on practice;

(viii) appropriate expertise on the part of higher education institutions and other providers of INSET;

(ix) appropriate preparatory and follow-up work in schools.

Later, attention is turned to the planning and implementation of INSET in schools and it is here that the annual cycle of INSET planning, which has more recently become usual practice in LEAs and schools, is advocated. The stages from needs identification through prioritization and the choice of training activities to the monitoring and evaluation of training are demarcated.

Heralding the pattern of LEA funding that was to be introduced a year later in TRIST and subsequently in LEATGS (the Local Education Authority Training Grants Scheme) it is stated that: 'We believe that the main role of the LEA should be to decide on its priorities for and policies towards INSET in the light of regional and national priorities, to set a budget for INSET and to allocate funds between the different types of activity in the light of its own priorities and the needs identified by the schools in the area' (para. 58). However, their recommendation concerning the amount of funding to be available to LEAs for INSET has not been implemented. They suggested that 'it would be reasonable for that target to be equivalent to about 5% of LEAs' expenditure on teachers' salaries or about £210 m. at 1983–84 prices', and they acknowledged that for the majority of LEAs this would seem likely to imply a substantial increase in INSET funding.

Another area discussed in the report which has not been implemented is the establishment of a regional planning structure for INSET. At the heart of this proposal was the concept of 'brokerage'. 'The main function of the new mechanism would be to act as a "broker" in securing a match between the INSET needs of LEAs which could not be met adequately from within their own provision and the INSET provision made by higher education institutions including award-bearing courses' (para. 67). They saw some 20 area committees being set up in England and Wales, with their membership being drawn from LEAs, higher education institutions and local teachers. As we shall see later, this proposal was not included in the LEATGS arrangements, although the possibility of a regional structure was contemplated in the TRIST scheme.

Central to any improvement in the provision of INSET was the availability of adequate funds. With regard to this the report referred to the role of higher education and recommended that institutions of higher education should continue to receive substantial central funding, as provided since the introduction of the special arrangements in Circular 3/83, for INSET courses and other activities of one term or more full-time, or the part-time equivalent.

It was this report that provided the source of guidance for LEAs and schools in establishing the infrastructural and financial arrangements for developing INSET. It crystallized thinking and enabled providers, including higher education institutions, LEA INSET planners and senior staff in schools, to see where they might be located in a new system of INSET. What was required was a governmental response to the recommendations written into this policy document. This response came, rather surprisingly, not from the DES but from the Manpower Services Commission (MSC). The TVEI Unit within the MSC launched the TVEI Related In-Service Training Scheme (TRIST) for schools and teachers in further education in 1985.

TRIST April 1985 to April 1987

In April 1985, LEAs were invited to submit proposals by 24 June 1985 for INSET funding for the academic year 1985–86. It is important to note the short period given for the proposals to be formulated and submitted, since such a contracted time-scale has become a feature of INSET planning since then. Two other submission deadlines were given: 14 October 1985 for funding for the period January to September 1986 (or January 1986 to March 1987) and 24 January 1986 for the period April or September 1986 to March 1987.

The scheme was not comprehensive in scope since it was limited to teachers of young people in the age group 14–18, i.e. the sector directly related to TVEI. However, it did apply to schools and colleges other than those directly involved in the

TVEI pilot studies and it did include all subjects in the curriculum of schools and colleges.

It was important politically for TRIST to be seen as an interim, enabling scheme, bridging the gap between the publication of the ACSET report and the introduction of the LEA Training Grants Scheme. It was not a monopoly scheme since other funding arrangements, e.g. funding from the DES pool, continued through the TRIST period. TRIST was designed to stimulate new and/or additional in-service training and professional development. It was the novelty of provision that attracted some planners and providers but the new planning arrangements were also important.

In the document describing the arrangements for TRIST (Manpower Services Commission 1985) there are details of the scope of the scheme, including the eligible areas of training and methods of training. The areas of training need that would qualify for financial support were:

1. Training in relevant areas of the curriculum, especially in the shortage areas of CDT, technology, information technology, microelectronics, business studies and physical science.
2. Training to advance further practical, relevant teaching for students of all abilities and both sexes across all areas of the curriculum.
3. Training in new teaching approaches designed to increase the student's responsibility for his or her own learning.
4. Training in assessment, including both formal assessment and 'profiling' on the basis of regular assessment of students' progress and development.
5. Training in the organizational and management skills necessary to provide a more relevant, broad and balanced curriculum, including the application of subjects across the curriculum to working and adult life.
6. Training in the organization and operation of links between schools and colleges.
7. Training to enhance students' economic awareness and understanding of industry and commerce, including improved careers guidance.
8. Training and experience to encourage the mutual understanding,

17

and bringing together, of the needs of employers and the aims of schools and colleges.

9. Training in how to plan, integrate, supervise and evaluate work experience, industrial and commercial visits and residential experience.

10. Training to promote understanding of necessary changes in vocational courses and qualifications, taking account, where colleges are concerned, of new teaching approaches in schools.

11. Training in the management of curriculum and organizational change.

In the preparation of their proposals LEAs were required to show that they had planned a balanced programme that took account of the various areas of training and indicated how the proposed TRIST programme fitted into the LEA's overall training approach. LEAs also received guidance on the range of training activities that were suitable for the scheme. This range included the following:

1. Training programmes of substantial length to re-train or up-date teachers and lecturers in specific subjects – particularly in the shortage areas of CDT, technology, IT (information technology), business studies, micro-electronics, and physical science.

2. School- and college-based training, drawing on experienced teachers in schools and colleges, lecturers and consultants from higher education institutions, industry and commerce, to give teachers opportunities to develop and practise new teaching approaches.

3. Secondments to industry and commerce and, conversely, secondments from industry and commerce to schools and colleges.

4. Group work in other schools, on employers' premises, in colleges or in teachers' centres, including the development of mini-companies.

5. Exchanges with other schools and colleges and as appropriate with line managers in companies to learn about the management of resources and the expectations and requirements of employers.

6. LEA based courses provided by peripatetic staff using suitably equipped mobile teaching units.

7. Distance learning.

The attention paid to programmes and activities, rather than to the conventional provision of courses, is a striking feature of this list. Equally noticeable is the close link that is advocated between schools and the wider community, especially the industrial and commercial community. This latter comes as no surprise given the sponsorship of the scheme by TVEI.

Having specified the areas for training and suggested possible methods of provision, the TRIST planners went on to inform LEAs that they were expected to monitor and evaluate the INSET activities they mounted as part of the scheme. LEAs were expected to ensure that the provision was of high quality, focused on practice, followed up and translated into effective action, and that it offered value for money.

For funding purposes LEAs were grouped into four bands, as shown in Table 1.1. In addition to the maximum amount against which an LEA could frame its proposals there was an additional source of funding. Supplementary support was available for especially innovative proposals that were likely to be of regional or national importance.

LEAs falling in the following bands	Size of pupil/student/ client/group (secondary age pupils and 16–18 students in non-advanced further education)	Grant ceilings per authority (£)
1	0–33,000	150,000
2	33,000–66,000	300,000
3	66,000–100,000	450,000
4	100,000 +	600,000

Table 1.1 Local education authority bands

LEAs were expected to prepare their proposals in the short space of two months. In that time they needed to identify a person to be responsible for drafting the final proposal, to negotiate with colleges and schools and with providers and to gain the support of the elected members. The proposals needed to be costed and located in the existing INSET structures and plans.

LEAs were required to submit a training plan which included the following:

1. The overall objectives of the programme and how it complements other INSET activities of the authority.
2. The particular INSET needs to be addressed within it.
3. How the teachers to be given training are to be identified and selected and the use to be made of their expertise following training.
4. The projected numbers of school and FE teachers to receive training.
5. The courses or arrangements to be used, showing existing and proposed courses separately.
6. The monitoring and evaluating arrangements.
7. How the training provided might be part of a continuing process of professional development of the teachers concerned.
8. The management arrangements for delivery of the programme.
9. A summary of costs requested.

It is remarkable how responsive LEAs and providers were to this initiative. They demonstrated that they were able to produce the necessary documentation in order to receive their allocation of funds. What is even more remarkable is what was achieved in the short life of TRIST. The word TRIST passed quickly into the language of secondary schools, highlighting the changing status of INSET in school organization and planning. At LEA and school levels new titles were given to staff and TRIST co-ordinators could be identified in the advisory staffs of LEAs and in the senior management of secondary schools. These co-ordinators became parts of networks operating at local, regional and national levels. The notion of consortia that embraced schools and colleges in local areas and clusters of specialists drawn from regions or across the country became familiar. Innovatory INSET activities were pioneered, including technology buses, distance learning packages and new types of course activity, often based in comfortable country hotels. Much attention was given to the dissemination of good practice and national TRIST publications were given wide circulation. In addition, local and regional publications were produced. Close attention was paid to the evaluation of TRIST at school, LEA and national levels. In later chapters I shall return to some of the features of TRIST, including evaluation in Chapter 7. When TRIST came to an end in 1987 it was followed by a string of publications that document its achievements. These publications include a directory of TRIST practice containing abstracts of a large number of TRIST reports, and papers produced by schools, colleges, LEAs and regional groups, a series of papers of national interest and a number of national evaluation reports.

GRIST to LEATGS

The White Paper *Better Schools* (DES/Welsh Office 1985a) gave notice of the Government's intention to bring forward legislation to introduce a new specific grant to support LEA expenditure on most aspects of in-service training. It states:

Individual teachers need support and encouragement for their professional development at all stages of their career:
* newly trained teachers need structured support and guidance during probation and their early years in the profession;
* other newly appointed and promoted teachers, not least those appointed to headships, need to be able to draw upon induction and training programmes directly relevant to their new tasks and responsibilities;
* all teachers need help in assessing their own professional performance and in building on their strengths and working on the limitations identified;
* all teachers need to be able to engage in in-service training relevant to their teaching and professional needs.

In September 1985 the DES circulated a letter to a number of bodies, although it was intended principally for representatives of LEAs, such as the Association of County Councils and the Association of Metropolitan Authorities, which carried the title 'Specific grant arrangements to support the inservice training of teachers'. With the letter came a position paper, prepared by the DES and the Welsh Office, which set out the issues that arose in introducing a specific grant to LEAs for INSET:

scope of specific grant arrangements;

expenditure to be supported;
scheme of grants;
rate of grants;
indicative allocation of grants;
audit arrangements;
monitoring and evaluation;
administration;
relationship with the TRIST scheme;
timing of the new arrangements;
fee policy;
the future of the INSET pool;
course approval;
INSET provision in HE institutions;
regional co-ordination of INSET;
relationship with other existing specific grants.

A great deal of consultation took place in the following months and almost a year later, on 29 August, the DES published Circular 6/86, *Local Education Authority Training Grants Scheme: Financial Year 1987–88*. The scheme was christened GRIST (Grant Related In-Service Training) although it is now usually referred to as LEATGS, keeping to the initials used in the Circular. The main purposes of the new scheme were to support expenditure on INSET so as: 'to promote the professional development of teachers; to promote more systematic and purposeful planning of in-service training; to encourage more effective management of the training force; and to encourage training in selected areas, which are to be accorded national priority' (para. 4).

There were two categories of grants: grants related to DES determined national priorities, which were supported at a 70 per cent rate; and grants related to locally assessed needs and priorities, which were supported at a 50 per cent rate. LEAs were listed and they were each given indicative allocations for grant in relation to the national priorities. Each LEA was required to submit proposals to the DES/Welsh Office for funding a programme of INSET, which covered expenditure up to the indicative allocation. The scheme applied to teachers in .

schools and further, higher and adult education, youth and community workers, educational psychologists, and LEA inspectors and advisers. In 1987–88 the sum of £200 million was made available for the scheme, of which £70 million was ear-marked for the national priorities. LEAs were encouraged to monitor and evaluate the implementation of the scheme. They were also expected to collaborate with each other, providers in higher education and elsewhere, industry and commerce, Regional Advisory Councils and relevant voluntary bodies. LEAs were required to base their planning arrangements on the expressed needs and views of teachers, schools, colleges and other eligible groups. LEAs were requested to submit their proposals by 17 October 1986 and it was intended that they would be informed of their grant aid by 19 December 1987, so that they could begin implementing their plans in the financial year commencing April 1987. This cycle of planning and expenditure has become familiar since 1986.

The basic pattern of LEATGS has remained unchanged although the national priorities have been reviewed annually. The lists of these priorities for the first year of LEATGS and for 1990–91 are reproduced below:

Local Education Authority Training Grants Scheme: Financial Year 1987–88

National priority areas for school-teachers

1. Training in organization and management in the context of the responsibilities of headteachers and other senior teachers in schools.
2. Training in the teaching of mathematics.
3. Training to meet the special educational needs of pupils with learning difficulties in schools.
4. Training related to industry, the economy and the world of work.
5. Training in the teaching of science.
6. Training in the teaching of craft, design and technology.
7. Training in teaching and the planning of the curriculum in a multi-ethnic society.
8. Training in the teaching of microelectronics and in the use of microelectronics across the curriculum.
9. Training in the teaching of religious education.
    [Items 10–15 relate to further education teachers]

16. Training for the General Certificate of Secondary Education (GCSE).
17. Training to help combat the misuse of drugs.

Local Education Authority Training Grants Scheme: Financial Year 1990-91
National priority areas for school-teachers
1. Training in organization and management relating to the responsibilities of head teachers and other senior teachers in schools.
2. Training in schoolteacher appraisal.
3A. Training for the basic curriculum and collective worship.
3B. Designated courses in the teaching of primary mathematics.
3C. Designated courses in the teaching of primary science.
4. Training in the teaching of children in primary classes who are younger than 'rising five'.
5. Training to meet the special educational needs of pupils who have disabilities of hearing.
6. Training to meet the special educational needs of pupils who have disabilities of sight.
7. Training to meet the educational needs of pupils who have severe learning difficulties.
8. Training for designated teachers to meet special educational needs in ordinary schools.
9. Training in the use of new technologies across the curriculum.
10. Training for licensed and articled teachers.
11. Training in the management of pupils' behaviour.
   [Items 12–17 relate to further education teachers]

18. Training in various aspects of preventative health education.

The bridge between TRIST and LEATGS lies in the annual cycle of planning and implementation, which has required LEAs and schools to develop appropriate structures for meeting externally imposed requirements. This annual cycle has been criticized by LEAs, who have argued that it is difficult to make medium term and long term plans for INSET since there is no guarantee of funding for particular activities and priorities. INSET providers also express concern about the cycle although they are even more concerned about the increasing focus of LEA funding on INSET activities that are LEA provided. The ending of the pool saw a sharp reduction in teacher secondments to long courses and an increase in short *ad hoc* training. Much of the innovative collaborative work undertaken with TRIST funds has a lower profile, as LEAs have lost access to regional funding. It is the strong LEA focus that is the most distinctive feature of LEATGS.

Review

There can be little doubt that since 1986 INSET has become a much more noticeable feature of the education system in England and Wales. Not only is there a new cadre of INSET co-ordinators in LEAs and schools, there is also a range of new consultative and planning bodies. There are new persons, structures and processes. These *needed* to be in place given the speed and extent of educational change since 1987. We have witnessed a very brief consultative stage before the passing of the Education Reform Act of 1988. For some LEAs, the lessons learned from the INSET 'cascade' programme for the introduction of the General Certificate of Secondary Education (GCSE) are being used to cope with the massive retraining requirements associated with, among other things, reforms of the curriculum, pupil assessment, teacher appraisal and local school management. TRIST and GRIST had increased teachers' expectations for improved professional development. ACSET had emphasized the need for a balance to be struck between the personal and professional needs of individual teachers and the needs of functional groups and whole schools. Achieving this balance in the light of externally determined priorities is one of the most pressing issues in contemporary INSET planning. The way LEAS and schools have adapted to the changing circumstances is the focus of the succeeding chapters.

2 Local education authorities and INSET

As was indicated in the previous chapter, local education
authorities have established a number of different arrangements
for providing INSET for the teachers in their employment. This
element of difference is the essence of any attempt to describe
what goes on within LEAs. Any attempt to define a pattern is
distinguished by the looseness of the generalizations: when it
comes to specifics each LEA must be treated as a separate case.
The variety can be accounted for in a number of ways, including
location, geographical size, demography, economic structure,
political party allegiance, social structure and educational
history. The result of this variety is that any attempt by central
government to impose a uniform pattern yields a mixed
response. The stronger the arguments for pupils' entitlement to a
common curriculum and for teachers' entitlement to continuing
professional development, the greater is the need for more
uniformity of provision.

The recognition of this need for greater uniformity can be
found in curriculum documents associated with the Great Debate. At the very outset of that debate the DES laid out its agenda
for public discussion in its paper *Educating Our Children:
Four Subjects for Debate* (DES 1977), which included a brief section titled 'Acceptable and unacceptable diversity'. This begins:

> In being concerned to secure certain educational essentials for all
> children, we should not reject all diversity. There is some diversity that
> legitimately can cause worry: as families move about the country,
> parents are right to be concerned if they encounter lack of continuity in
> their children's education. We need to recognize that not all differences
> are harmful and some may be positively beneficial. (para. 2.13)

For our purposes, the key role of adequately prepared teachers in providing the curriculum is of most relevance. As was stated later in the same document (para. 2.17): 'Assisting the schools, by means of both initial and in-service training, to acquire the teachers they need is a necessary corollary of specifying curricular requirements. By the same token, only when curricular needs are more clearly defined and agreed can the training system effectively play its part'.

In 1977 the DES sent a questionnaire to all the LEAs in England and Wales seeking information about their curriculum policies. Two-thirds of the authorities stated that they 'had not established, and would not wish to see develop, a formal system of detailed control over the curriculum of individual schools' (DES 1979).

In 1981 the DES reminded LEAs that:

> The Education Acts lay on local education authorities the responsibility of securing the provision of efficient and sufficient primary and secondary education to meet the needs of their areas. . . . To fulfil their responsibilities effectively within a national framework, authorities have to exercise leadership for their areas and interpret national policies and objectives in the light of local needs and circumstances. . . . Local authorities thus have a responsibility to formulate curricular policies and objectives which meet national policies and objectives, command local assent, and can be applied by each school to its own circumstances (paras 8 and 9).

In Section 17 of the Education (No. 2) Act 1986, this acquired the force of law. It was stated that:

1. It shall be the duty of every local education authority –
   (a) to determine and keep under review, their policy in relation to the secular curriculum for the county, voluntary and special schools maintained by them;
   (b) to make and keep up to date, a written statement of that policy; and
   (c) to furnish the governing body and head teacher of every such school with a copy of the statement and publish it in such other manner as the authority consider appropriate.

As was highlighted at the end of Chapter 1, 1986 was the year when the Circular (6/86) announcing the commencement of new funding arrangements for INSET (GRIST) appeared. The matching of formal LEA curriculum policies to formal INSET policies was a major task for LEAs in the summer of that year. There were four main purposes of the GRIST scheme: 'to promote the professional development of teachers; to promote more systematic and purposeful planning of in-service training; to encourage more effective management of the teacher force; to encourage training in selected areas, which are to be accorded national priority'.

LEAs were invited to submit proposals for expenditure of the grants under specific headings. It was necessary for them to demonstrate that they had comprehensive INSET plans which took into account local and national priorities, which specified the methods of delivery, including collaborative arrangements, and which incorporated monitoring and evaluation. Funds were available within GRIST for establishing and maintaining the INSET infrastructures within LEAs. I have already referred to the developing structure of advisory support and teachers' centres as important components of the infrastructures of some, if not most, LEAs. In Circular 6/86 six categories of eligible expenditure were listed and two of these had infrastructural consequences for LEAs. One was concerned with the costs of providing or evaluating INSET, these costs including part of the salaries of those specifically employed to provide, support or evaluate INSET. The other concerned relevant costs incurred in providing and maintaining premises for INSET. This provided encouragement and the means for LEAs to strengthen their advisory and teacher support teams and to improve the availability of teachers' centres. For the purpose of GRIST the priorities included appraising the appropriateness of the structures put in place for TRIST, and for some LEAs the introduction of TVEI, and either reinforcing those structures or establishing new ones.

For all the LEAs the essential tasks remained the same: establishing appropriate consultation arrangements, identifying

INSET needs, prioritizing them and attributing financial estimates to those which would be met, designing a strategic plan for implementation, implementing the plan and monitoring and evaluating both the INSET activities generated by the plan and the total INSET policy-making, planning and implementation system. All LEAs and INSET providers had to work to the deadlines indicated in Figure 2.1. LEAs received the INSET Circular and then needed to prepare their plans, send

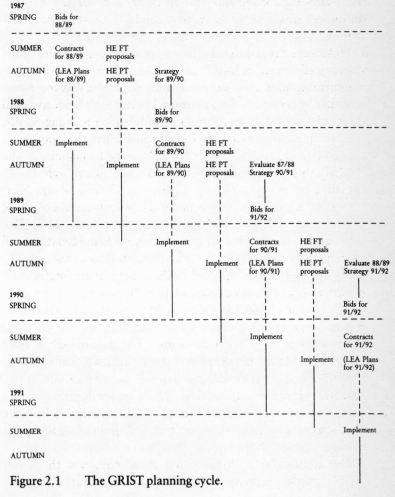

Figure 2.1   The GRIST planning cycle.

them to the DES for scrutiny, after approval implement the plans and then monitor and evaluate them. No sooner had they begun the first implementation cycle than they had to start the next planning cycle. LEAs argued that they were unable to plan more than a year ahead since there was no guarantee that national priorities would remain fixed for any length of time, and there was too much fluidity in the education system, with reform of examinations such as GCSE, the introduction of TVEI, and the managerial and teaching implications of the Education Reform Act to take into account.

To illustrate some of the structural responses made by LEAs to the changing demands being placed upon them for systematically planned INSET, I have chosen three LEAs from whom information was gathered from documentation and by interview. In collecting the information the LEAs were advised that in any published account they would remain anonymous. Two of the LEAs are metropolitan counties and the third is a shire county.

Example 1

The first LEA to be considered is a large shire county. Here the drawing up of the first INSET plan submitted to the DES as part of the GRIST proposals had been the responsibility of the Chief Adviser. In 1987 the LEA appointed a principal adviser (INSET and curriculum) whose special responsibilities lay in the co-ordination of specialist and cross-curriculum advisers, overseeing the training of teachers and preparing the annual GRIST submission. The place of the principal adviser in the staffing hierarchy within the LEA is shown in Figure 2.2.

As can be seen, the principal adviser worked closely with senior advisers, district advisers and curriculum advisers, together with administrative staff at county and district levels. Given the size of this LEA's area and the administrative structures inherited with local government reorganization in 1974, it was necessary for the LEA to divide the county into six districts, and these were the working bases for the district

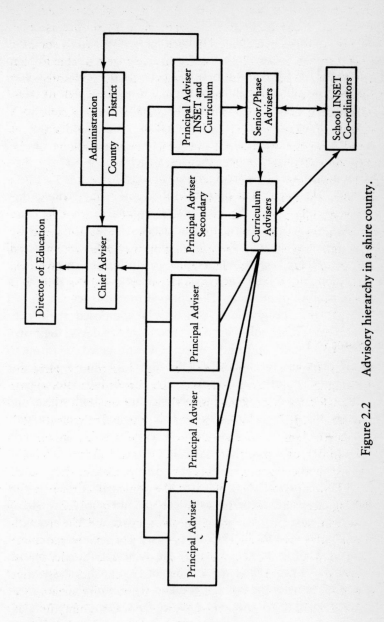

Figure 2.2   Advisory hierarchy in a shire county.

advisers. Across the county there were two professional resource centres and two teachers' centres. GRIST funding enabled the LEA to plan for locating a professional resource centre in each of the six districts.

From TRIST the LEA inherited a network of secondary school INSET co-ordinators. In each school a member of staff at senior level had taken on this post, usually as an additional responsibility, and these co-ordinators retained this responsibility under GRIST. All schools were required by the LEA to produce staff development policies, which would describe their arrangements for identifying training needs.

Once the needs had been identified school by school, they were discussed with the LEA phase – primary, secondary and further – advisers and district advisers. This information was then considered at county level, thus enabling the principal adviser (INSET and curriculum) to prioritize needs. The provision of INSET activities to meet the needs was a responsibility of advisers. They helped to construct the annual LEA INSET programme, which was composed mainly of short courses. Schools were also encouraged to devise their own training activities and LEA guidance was provided in writing to assist them in this. Before GRIST this LEA had seconded a substantial number of teachers to attend full-time award-bearing courses in higher education institutions, both within and outside the county boundaries. This secondment programme ceased in 1987, although some teachers were still able to obtain financial support to attend part-time courses in institutions of higher education.

The LEA sought to establish a balance between the needs of individual teachers, the needs of schools, the needs of districts and the needs of the LEA as a whole. Some finance had been devolved to schools. In 1987 all primary and secondary schools received £50 per teacher for the year, which could be spent on what the LEA called establishment initiated schemes. In addition, some of the larger secondary schools received an extra member of staff to provide supply cover for teachers attending INSET activities in school time.

Before GRIST this LEA had a consultative INSET committee, which was chaired by an administrative officer and drew its membership from the LEA advisory staff, representatives of teachers' unions, wardens of teachers' centres and representatives of institutions of higher education. There was also a member responsible for liaison with other LEAs through links with a neighbouring INSET consortium of metropolitan LEAs.

Inevitably in an LEA of this size there were difficulties in communication and co-ordination. The communication problem existed at a number of levels, e.g. vertically and horizontally between different advisers, between advisers in general and district staff, between the LEA centrally and individual schools. Breakdowns in communication found expression in weaknesses in co-ordination. These were intensified by the shortness of the timescales demanded by the one-year planning and implementation cycles of GRIST.

Example 2

This metropolitan LEA had established an INSET team comprising an INSET adviser, an INSET co-ordinator, general advisers, INSET consultants, TVEI personnel, an evaluator, technicians and a financial and staffing administration assistant. Most of the team were located in a former secondary school, which had been converted into a professional development centre and which contained conference rooms, offices and a resources centre. It housed a number of support staff associated with projects funded by Education Support Grants (ESGs). In another former school the LEA had a teachers' centre, which had been set up before TRIST. It is interesting to note the division of responsibilities between an INSET adviser and an INSET co-ordinator. Their positions in the staffing hierarchy are shown in Figure 2.3.

The INSET adviser had been appointed with the introduction of GRIST and had specific responsibilities for strategic planning in close consultation with advisers and school-based INSET

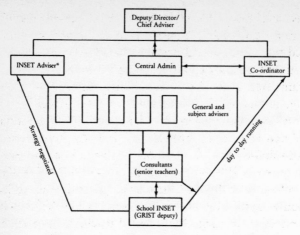

Figure 2.3   The place of an INSET adviser and an INSET
               co-ordinator in an LEA hierarchy.

co-ordinators. The INSET co-ordinator had been appointed
initially as the LEA's TRIST co-ordinator and was responsible
for the detailed planning and delivery of INSET. This person
had specific responsibility for co-ordinating the work of a small
group of consultants and for the day-to-day running of the
professional development centre. In the latter he was assisted by
the clerical, secretarial and technical staff who had been
appointed using GRIST funds.

In this LEA the major thrusts in the INSET plan were the
movement towards a school-based and school-focused model
and the appointment of specialist consultants on secondment
from local schools. To support school initiatives each school
was allocated for the school year 1987–88 a sum of £200
plus £10 per teacher and there was some enhancement to school
staffing. Thus, all the secondary schools in the LEA were
allocated an extra scale point and these were awarded to
teachers who took over some of the responsibilities undertaken
by deputy headteachers for TRIST. In addition, all primary and
secondary schools were given a 0.5 staffing enhancement to
provide some cover for teachers engaged in INSET activities.
The importance given to the school as the location for INSET is

indicated in Figure 2.4, which shows the estimated GRIST expenditure for this LEA. Notice the proportion of the total funds allocated to give support to teachers in schools in such fields as information technology and teaching/learning strategies. The consultants had a number of functions, including negotiating, planning, preparing, delivering and evaluating INSET sessions for whole schools, departments, functional groups, individual teachers and clusters of schools. In 1987–88 there were three such consultants and the authority planned to increase the number to ten in 1988–89 and fifteen in 1989–90. The absence of any reference to finance for teacher secondments to higher education is significant in this authority, which before GRIST had seconded a substantial number of teachers annually. Some secondments were allowed for in the GRIST budget but these were increasingly seen as opportunities for teachers to engage in tasks relevant to the LEA's policies.

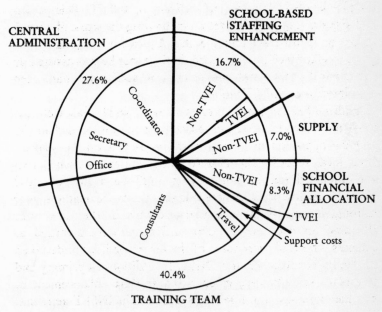

Figure 2.4   Allocation of INSET funding in a metropolitan LEA.

The LEA provided the schools with a planning framework for INSET and guidance on how to draw up an INSET and staff development programme. Schools were encouraged to establish staff development committees led by INSET co-ordinators. They were expected to consult advisers. The advisers assisted in building the school plans into the authority's annual plan. The schools were also expected to monitor all school-based INSET using a pro-forma and to summarize this information twice a year in a report submitted to the authority. They were also expected to evaluate on an annual basis their INSET programmes. Interestingly, this LEA seconded a teacher as a full-time evaluator. This scheme had been introduced under TRIST, with a two-year secondment followed by another appointment under GRIST.

This LEA had devised a clear policy for its INSET activities, including the establishment of a hierarchical infrastructure headed by a senior member of staff in the LEA – the deputy director – who played an active role in the system. Experience of TRIST had demonstrated the worth of appointing specialist consultants and these were seen as an essential part of a school-based model of INSET planning and delivery. Inevitably, there were variations in the competence and expertise of the consultants. The pattern was to appoint teachers who had recently successfully completed a period of secondment to an institution of higher education. As experts they worked sometimes as a team but more often alone. It was evident that they were unable to meet all the demands made upon them. Striking a balance between helping individual teachers in particular schools and helping large numbers of teachers within the authority was a difficult problem for them. I shall return to the role of consultants in Chapter 6.

Example 3

In this metropolitan LEA there was an INSET management team headed by an assistant director of education who was responsible for staffing and curriculum. The advisory staff were staff were at the heart of the INSET planning and delivery arrangements. As can be seen in Figure 2.5 the advisers were, in the eyes of the assistant director, located at different levels within the LEA hierarchy.

The management team comprised the assistant director, an INSET co-ordinator, a senior adviser, advisers, a staff development centre warden, members of the LEA support staff and administrative staff. The advisers met as a group once a week to exchange information and discuss current issues, which

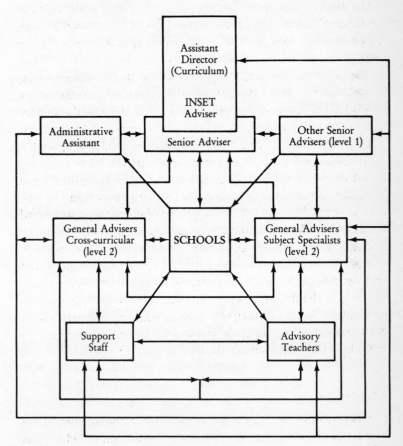

Figure 2.5   INSET structure in an LEA.

were largely INSET related. The advisers were divided according to seniority and also by function. Although they were all described as general advisers, some were subject specialists and others had cross-curricular responsibilities. Each adviser had pastoral and liaison responsibilities for designated schools. The support staff included seconded teachers working on LEA-initiated curriculum development projects, ESG projects and projects funded from Section 11 funding, the last related to the special provisions made for LEAs having substantial numbers of pupils from overseas.

The LEA had a staff development centre and a curriculum development centre and these were serviced by secretarial and administrative staff funded by GRIST. There were also a number of specialist development centres, e.g. a multi-cultural support centre. One of these centres was a converted secondary school that was also a resources centre. This LEA had been able to use GRIST funds, and, for TVEI, Extension funds to enlarge its advisory services.

The implications of GRIST for the LEA's INSET policy can be seen in the two diagrams in Figure 2.6. There are significant reductions in the allocation of funds for award-bearing courses in higher education institutions, for LEA provided courses and for short courses provided elsewhere. More funds have been allocated to national initiatives and in-school INSET.

To encourage schools to develop their own INSET policies all schools in the LEA were allocated £200 plus £20 per teacher per year in 1987. In addition each school received 30 'supply days' for school-determined INSET and each secondary school received 40 'supply days' to be spent on INSET associated with the introduction of the new GCSE examinations.

Before TRIST and GRIST the LEA was very aware of its small advisory service and the difficulties of providing appropriate support for teachers with specialist interests, especially teachers in secondary schools. To try to alleviate the problems money had been allocated to groups of teachers, who formed LEA-based specialist subject associations so that programmes could be arranged by the teachers themselves. These 20 or so

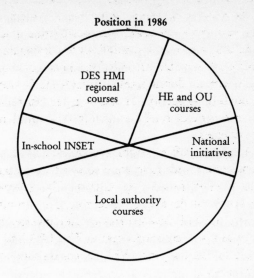

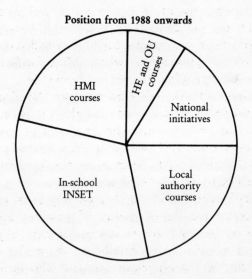

Figure 2.6   Changes in the allocation of INSET funds in an LEA.

associations were active in identifying needs and seeking to meet those needs through conferences, workshops and self-help activities. The success of the groups depended heavily upon the enthusiasm, energy and commitment of a small number of individuals. With the advent of TRIST each secondary school nominated a member of staff, usually a deputy head, as a staff development tutor and these persons continued to keep their INSET responsibilities when GRIST arrived. They had been encouraged by the LEA to set up INSET committees in their schools.

Each school had been asked to establish five major priority training needs. The schools had not been advised what methods they should use to identify needs, although this LEA had a firm commitment to GRIDS (Guidelines for Review and Internal Development in Schools – a project initially funded by the Schools Council, to which I shall refer in Chapter 4) in the primary school sector, and some secondary schools were experimenting in using this approach. The identified priority areas would be the subject of discussion between each school's staff development tutor, the liaison adviser and the INSET co-ordinator. These people would be responsible for matching the school's identified needs with the overall INSET strategy of the LEA, which took into account national priorities and LEA-determined local priorities.

TRIST and GRIST had enabled this LEA to establish a new INSET infrastructure. In part, this was a tidying up operation, in that it brought a number of disparate activities together into a single system. New appointments, new consultative procedures, new buildings and material resources, new administrative support arrangements and new patterns of delivery all intensified interest in INSET and indicated the LEA's commitment to its teachers. Inevitably, these changes revealed difficulties in liaison between the support services and the schools and in co-ordination of school plans and the LEA's overall plans. Monitoring and evaluation were areas that required close attention. There was still an over-dependence on *ad hoc* courses designed by providers, although schools were learning alternative ways of meeting their needs, especially the use of their own staff expertise.

These three examples help to provide some insight into the ways LEAs responded to Circular 6/86. They bear out the list of issues produced by the evaluators of the LEA management aspects of TRIST (Hall and Oldroyd 1988):

- Managing INSET in a climate of uncertainty, e.g. about new and future legislation and conditions of service.
- Managing a multiplicity of innovations (e.g. TVEI extension, GRIST, work-related NAFE – non-advanced further education – ESGs), all requiring separate bids for staff development to be submitted at different times in the year.
- Managing the tensions at different points of the system, e.g. between DES and LEA, elected members and officers, LEA and schools and individual teachers.
- Establishing and supporting new professional development management roles and structures, e.g. advisory teachers and INSET management groups.
- Managing the changing role of the adviser, e.g. in setting budgets, managing often conflicting priorities, achieving credibility in dovetailing 'new' and 'old' INSET systems.
- Meeting the needs of those responsible for managing INSET.
- Creating, maintaining and monitoring financial structures to take account of new funding arrangements, including financial devolution of institutions.
- Managing widespread consultation in a way that keeps all participants involved but reconciles conflicting interests.
- Ensuring good communication within and between different levels in the LEA, including the dissemination of INSET outcomes.
- Identifying needs, distinguishing between needs and wants, and dealing with raised teacher expectations.
- Achieving a balance between individual, group, institutional, LEA and national needs.
- Managing the relationship with a new range of providers.
- Getting the best from external providers.
- Devising alternative professional development programmes which go beyond the traditional in-service workshop and include achieving a balance between institution-based and off-site activities.

- Arranging professional development programmes which are at times and locations which make them accessible to all and avoid disruption to pupil learning.
- Creating and maintaining regional support networks between LEAs without overlap.
- Monitoring the implementation of the INSET programme in schools across the LEA.
- Evaluating the impact of professional development programmes on staff and pupils.
- Balancing the breadth of provision required to meet the needs of a wide range of people with the depth needed for major impact on practice within a limited budget.

It would be easy to suggest that LEAs have been unable to rise to meet fully the challenges that have come with new funding arrangements. To do so would be to ignore the difficulties that LEAs have had to face as they have been required to respond to a variety of changes that have been forced upon them by both internal and external pressures. Advisers describe themselves more as firefighters than as architects. Many who were initially appointed to the advisory service from schools, as subject specialists or phase specialists, have seen their job definitions extended to take on more and more school pastoral responsibilities and increasing administrative duties. School reorganization and rationalization as a result of demographic changes, implementing a series of government education acts which have had major implications for school organization and management and for the education of groups of children (e.g. children with special education needs and children from ethnic minorities), introducing TVEI and a number of curriculum proposals stemming from government reports (e.g. Bullock, Cockcroft, Swann and Warnock) and HMI discussion papers (e.g. the Matters for Discussion series) – all these have made demands on advisory staffs at a time when pressure was on LEAs to reduce their staffing. More recently, the Education Reform Act of 1988 has resulted in a redefinition of the relationship between LEAs and schools. The strengthening of school governing bodies is being achieved at the expense of a reduction in the role of the LEAs. For LEA advisers and inspectors, who have been at the sharp end of INSET planning and provision, this has led to a reappraisal of their roles. As HMI (1989b), in their report on the first year of LEATGS, commented:

> The role of established inspectors and advisers is changing with fewer having control of INSET budgets and more becoming managers of INSET rather than providers. This change of role, allied with the new appointments made, has created tensions, frustrations and uncertainties within the advisory services of some LEAs. By the end of the first year LEAs were beginning to review the management and structure of their advisory/inspectorate services to ensure that they were better placed to meet the various new challenges, of which LEATGS was but one.

In the same report HMI comment on the slowness of the development of inter-LEA collaboration. This had been one of the thrusts of TRIST, and was continued into GRIST and LEATGS. It had been highlighted in Circular 6/86 in the statement: 'authorities need to collaborate with each other to ensure as effective planning and delivery as possible of training for which individual authorities are likely to have insufficient resources or expertise, or limited local demand'. Despite this encouragement it was clear that LEATGS had reinforced the tradition within LEAs of defining INSET relatively tightly inside their own boundaries. Even with funds being provided specifically for inter-LEA collaborative initiatives in the TRIST scheme, it was noticeable how few inter-LEA activities there were. As part of the TRIST dissemination exercise a Paper of National Interest (Williams and England 1988) was written to draw attention to the place of inter-LEA collaboration in TRIST. We noted that 'For LEAs, key issues include the substance of any collaboration, the appropriate LEAs with which to collaborate, their location, and the nature and extent of the collaboration'. We illustrated the potential contact points between LEAs, as shown in Table 2.1.

In response to the statement in *Arrangements for the TVEI Related In-Service Training Scheme (England and Wales)*

(Manpower Services Commission 1985), which welcomed inter-LEA collaboration, 22 projects were initiated.

LEA A	LEA B
1. LEA officers and advisers ←→	1. LEA officers and advisers
2. LEA projects, e.g. TVEI and ESG groups ←→	2. LEA projects, e.g. TVEI and ESG groups
3. Schools and colleges, including clusters and consortia ←→	3. Schools and colleges, including clusters and consortia
4. Individual teachers and groups of teachers ←→	4. Individual teachers and groups of teachers

Table 2.1 Potential contact points between local education authorities

Their titles are:

1. Designing designers.
2. Training and development of institution-based INSET co-ordinators.
3. LEA/provider co-ordination programme.
4. CDT – support through change.
5. A study of futures applied to the curriculum.
6. Modern languages into business.
7. Tameside and Rochdale equal opportunities programme.
8. Micro-electronics and music.
9. Modern language skills for work.
10. Modular curriculum.
11. INSET needs in information technology in Merseyside.
12. INSET co-ordinators.
13. Training information exchange.
14. Practical mechanics.
15. INSET for FE staff with responsibility for special needs.
16. New INSET arrangements: alternatives to courses.
17. Recording and accrediting the in-service training and development of individual teachers.
18. Support for innovation project.
19. Production of INSET video tapes.

20. Production of Welsh medium INSET materials.
21. Joint modular humanities initiative.
22. Open learning/self-supported study in schools.

When the directors of these projects were brought together, a list of advantages of inter-LEA collaboration for LEAs, on the one hand, and schools, colleges and teachers, on the other, was drawn up. For the LEAs the advantages were:

- Strengthening communication/liaison between specialist LEA advisers/managers.
- Sharing of experiences to sharpen up issues and inform planning.
- Gaining insight into other LEA approaches and styles of working with schools.
- Being able to compare and contrast different approaches to management and delivery of INSET and to identify effective practice in both.
- Being able to step outside LEA traditional ways of working and to innovate.
- Gaining status from larger scale projects.
- Gaining access to a wider range of resources, both human and material.
- Updating advisory staff and drawing their attention to modern practice in curriculum areas.
- Enabling resources to be pooled and so generating the provision of more and better INSET activities.
- Planning strategically with providers to give economies of scale in the management and delivery of INSET.
- Liaising with INSET providers simplifies their administration, marketing, etc., thus enabling providers to give a better service.

Many of these advantages for LEAs can be translated into advantages for schools, colleges and teachers.

- Exchanging ideas on a broader front.
- Enriching curriculum initiatives by joint INSET programmes in terms of curriculum and materials development, and disseminating to inform and support local activities.
- Organizing more easily relevant visits, exchanges, and participation in INSET projects. These are important to teachers in their current, less mobile, career pattern.

45

- Sharing of expertise and professional problems from which personal friendships and networks develop.
- Developing specialist networks of individuals and also of functional groups.
- Having access to different perceptions and modes of working which empower teachers and their schools to press for change.
- Aggregating sufficient numbers of teachers in shortage areas to achieve 'critical mass' and so obtain relevant INSET.
- Gaining wider opportunities for staff development.
- Widening of school/college horizons introduces new ideas and approaches to common and individual problems.
- Legitimating innovations enables teachers to step outside potential intra-LEA conflict.
- Raising the profile of a particular curriculum area or educational issue, e.g. gender.

Although the project directors had no difficulty in identifying these advantages they had also learned from their experience that there were three main areas of difficulty in initiating and sustaining inter-LEA collaboration: finance, administration and personal. To assist in overcoming these difficulties nine guidelines were suggested.

1. The appointment of regional INSET co-ordinators for groups of regionally related LEAs to facilitate collaboration across LEA boundaries. The following list of functions were included in the job description of a regional INSET co-ordinator appointed by the ten LEAs that were part of the now defunct Greater Manchester:
   (a) Dissemination of TRIST activities and in particular those involving more than one LEA.
   (b) Work with the ten Greater Manchester LEAs, co-ordinating those activities where inter-LEA co-operation is desirable.
   (c) Keep fully informed about all LEA INSET priorities and draw the attention of all participating LEAs to areas of common interest.
   (d) Develop strategies for co-operation with LEAs where there is agreement between them on the desirability of collaborative projects and liaise with groups of specialist advisers/consultants, etc., responsible for drawing up detailed schemes.
   (e) Ensure that individual LEAs are kept fully informed of the costs

of their participation in inter-LEA schemes so that adequate provision is made in their INSET budgets.

(f) Liaise with higher education institutions and with other providing bodies where appropriate and with inter-LEA co-ordinators in other regions.

(g) Keep the participating LEAs informed of new developments elsewhere.

(h) Draw up a database of provision in the participating LEAs of INSET materials and of expertise available so that LEAs may consider if they wish to draw on and purchase any such expertise not available within their own LEA.

(i) Present regular reports to the participating LEAs.

(j) Be responsible to a steering committee.

2. The establishment of internal structures within LEAs to foster and institutionalise collaboration and enhance its effectiveness. These include identification of INSET needs procedures which alerted teachers to the possibilities of receiving INSET in an inter-LEA context and the setting up of an efficient INSET communication network across LEAs in a region.

3. The establishment by LEAs of regional and sub-regional structures, e.g. regular meetings of LEA INSET advisers and other INSET managers and meetings between LEA advisory staff and INSET providers drawn from the same region.

4. The inclusion of inter-LEA collaboration within the job descriptions of key LEA decision-makers.

5. LEAs need to ensure that inter-LEA activities have a high profile in their strategic plans.

6. LEAs need to look closely at their administrative and, especially, financial cycles, to take account of possible collaboration.

7. LEAs need to provide for appropriate monitoring and evaluation strategies to ensure that any joint ventures are effective in meeting their goals.

8. LEAs need to identify teams of like-minded enthusiasts who may be trained for the management of inter-LEA projects since co-ordination of any project requires individuals with enthusiasm, conviction and commitment together with the necessary management skills to see a project through. It needs to be acknowledged that participation in collaborative projects is itself a valuable experience.

9. Effective inter-LEA projects are likely to require good dissemination

strategies, which are likely to include the preparation and distribution of good quality publications and the organization and provision of appropriate training activities.

Review

LEAs have been expected to make speedy responses to changes initiated by the DES in the funding of INSET. Not all of them had taken full advantage of pooling arrangements and what TRIST demonstrated was the considerable variety in structures and processes within LEAs for planning and providing INSET. From the examples quoted in this chapter, the different hierarchies created in LEAs can be seen. The introduction of TRIST saw the appointment of TRIST co-ordinators, usually from within the advisory staff, and many of these later became INSET advisers, who bear the responsibility for managing LEATGS. TRIST, GRIST and LEATGS required LEAs to demonstrate that they were able to plan INSET for teachers, psychologists, youth workers and others within their boundaries. LEAs have become increasingly expert in devising plan within tight time schedules and these plans take into account the identification of training needs, familiarity with national, local and school priorities, the location of appropriate expertise for INSET provision, and the application of methods of monitoring and evaluation. It is to the credit of LEAs that many of them have, in a relatively short period of time, established suitable structures, appointed specialist staff and devised a variety of procedures to facilitate a better provision for teachers. These procedures include needs identification, consultation as part of the planning process, the dissemination of information, negotiation with institutions of higher education and other providers, the provision of training activities, and the delegation of funds to individual schools. Not surprisingly, LEAs vary in their competence in each of these fields. This variety is one of the powerful reasons for establishing structures for inter-LEA collaboration. Such structures should provide for the dissemination of good practice and the sharing out of expertise in those areas where it is currently lacking.

3 Planning at school level

The shift from an essentially provider model to a school-based model of INSET has been one of the most striking trends in recent years in the provision of INSET in England and Wales. This is largely a reflection of changes in funding, although the conventions established through the involvement of schools in curriculum development projects, combined with the changing definition of the professional role of the teacher, played their part. This can be seen not only in the interaction between schools and teachers' centres but also in the responses of secondary schools to the possibility of devising and teaching their own externally accredited courses at CSE level (before the introduction of GCSE). Similarly, in primary schools, the freedom to engage in curriculum experimentation that followed the termination of 11+ testing contributed to these schools paying closer attention to their own curricular and school management arrangements. More recently, in secondary schools, the same emphasis on the response of the individual school to external initiatives can be seen in TVEI and its extension. For schools to take increasing responsibility for meeting the in-service needs of their teachers it has been necessary for changes to be made to the infrastructure of schools. Obtaining funds from the LEA may have been the motor for increasingly independent activity but for the motor to function properly, there needed to be some changes in the design of the vehicle.

In Figure 3.1 four aspects of school management are identified and shown to interact. The primary goal of a school in England and Wales is to interpret and provide the National Curriculum,

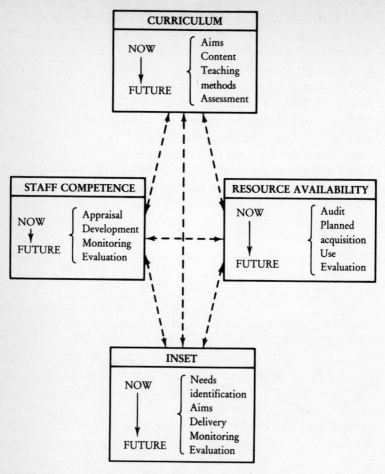

Figure 3.1   Interacting aspects of school management.

including the centrally defined core and foundation subjects, other subjects and cross-curricular themes. To provide the necessary curricular, extra-curricular and other activities a school has to pay close attention to the capabilities of the teaching staff and seek through staff development policies to manage the teaching resource effectively. Teachers require appropriate resources, including accommodation, curriculum materials and equipment, to enable them to achieve their own curricular and other goals. For teachers to keep abreast of their curricular interests provision must be made for INSET. A significant change in any one of the four areas shown in the boxes in Figure 3.1 results in changes in the other boxes. Change may start in any one of the boxes and lead to reactions in the others. At different times some areas will be largely responsive while others will be experiencing the introduction of a change stimulated from within or outside the school. This has implications for the managerial arrangement within schools. It suggests that decisions concerning INSET need to be made at those points in a school's organization where decisions about

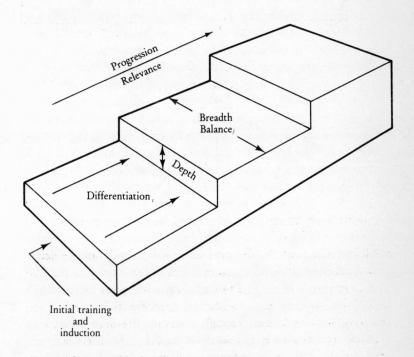

Figure 3.2   The INSET staircase.

resources, staff competence and curriculum are made. Before I turn to a consideration of some examples of the structural arrangements made within schools to facilitate the provision of appropriate INSET, some contextual matters need to be discussed.

INSET and teachers' careers

Reference has already been made in Chapter 1 to the three principal stages in a teacher's career: initial training, probation and induction, and continuing professional development. It is possible to draw an analogy between the main thread running through the Great Debate about the school curriculum and the 'curriculum' for the continuing professional development of teachers. The analogy is presented as a staircase in Figure 3.2.

Figure 3.2 highlights a number of important concepts: progression, relevance, differentiation, balance, breadth and depth. To assert the importance of progression in INSET is to downgrade the significance of disconnected *ad hoc* training events and to upgrade the sequencing of training events. This implies that INSET planners need to take close account of teachers' professional growth. In a teacher's career there are times when the need is for an introductory training experience, but this requires consolidation and further development. This is as true for the teacher who is in a stable curriculum-related post as it is for the teacher aspiring to gain promotion. Professional knowledge and skills need to be up-dated and enhanced regularly and, ideally, in a structured way. The arguments that the achievements of pupils ought to be monitored and recorded for both diagnostic and summative assessment purposes apply just as much to the professional growth of teachers.

It is easy to argue that all INSET should be relevant. Indeed it would appear to be so self-evident that comment is unnecessary. However, as soon as one asks the question, 'Relevant to what or whom?', it becomes clear that the concept of relevance is not straightforward: it is contentious. There can be a tension between the perceived needs of the individual teacher who seeks personal education and the needs of the school as a community. Many teachers give energy and time to their personal professional growth in order to leave the schools in which they are employed. Ambitious teachers seeking promotion to deputy headships and headships must usually change schools. Inevitably, there can be a conflict in what is required of those ambitious teachers between their employers, the staff of their current schools and the staff of schools to which they wish to move. There are other tensions within schools, e.g. between the demands of different roles that teachers are expected to play. Any teacher may be pulled between the needs to up-date subject knowledge, learn new subject-related skills, e.g. the effective use of information technology, become more competent in pupil assessment in the context of the National Curriculum, become familiar with the use of pupils' records of achievement, and so on. Not all these needs can be met in the short term. They must be prioritized and then met as part of a progressive, sequential training programme for each teacher. The relevance is partly determined by the external pressures and partly by internal school pressures. The critical question is what is relevant for each teacher at any moment. Who decides the priorities? The answer to this question is largely circumscribed by two different factors: the availability of resources to cover the costs of the training and the motivation, enthusiasm and availability of energy and time of the teacher.

This reference to some of the personal characteristics of the teacher underlies the importance of differentiation in INSET. Most teachers and providers have experienced the frustration and disappointment of participating in an INSET programme where it has been difficult to pitch the level of the activity because of the heterogeneity of the participants. It would appear to be axiomatic that any training activity should take account of the knowledge, skills and attitudes of the individual teachers about to undergo training. Yet so variable are teachers that it is extremely difficult to pitch training activities at the appropriate level to take account of individual differences. Teachers, like pupils, require individualized attention, but only rarely can this be provided. This is not to say that teachers do not make their own individual responses to any changes that are required of them or that they perceive to be necessary.

The introduction of the word balance is a reminder that attention must be paid by both the teacher and the school INSET planner to the tensions in the professional development of teachers. In any school year a teacher has only a small amount of time that can be devoted to his or her professional development. With the introduction of the National Curriculum in a series of stages laid out by the DES, teachers are able to envisage the years in which they are likely to be involved in some intense INSET activity. Figure 3.3 illustrates the build-up year-by-year of this introduction.

Programmes of study and assessment arrangements for each of the core and foundation subjects are becoming compulsory parts of schools' provision and to ensure their effective introduction all teachers require some preparation for the substantial changes. Not only must they be prepared to interpret and adapt the centrally determined substance of the changes – programmes of study and assessment – they must also modify their teaching and learning strategies. There are stages, from awareness arousal through the acquisition of appropriate knowledge, attitudes and skills, the introduction to the classroom, implementation and consolidation, to evaluation and revision, which must be undertaken by every teacher. It is obvious that teachers will come to these professional tasks differently. Any training programme ought, ideally, to take these differences into account. However, the temptation for LEAs and schools has been to discount these individual differences and to offer generalized programmes of INSET, usually as crash programmes as a response to short timescales. It is not simply that teachers require different programmes, it is also that close attention ought to be paid to the balance of pressures. Requirements stemming from the National Curriculum are not the only ones on the agenda for INSET. There are other aspects of school organization and management and the curricular life of schools that continue to be important. This can be seen most strikingly in the pastoral care and counselling aspects of school life. It can also be seen in the attention paid to the special education needs of a substantial number of pupils. Clearly, these considerations point to the importance of balance in INSET provision. Another dimension of the concept of balance is the distinction between what teachers require in the short term, the medium term and the longer term. Under increasing external pressures schools must focus sharply on the immediate issues requiring resolution. However, individual teachers may, in their career interests, focus simultaneously on the present and the future. Taking account of this time dimension in order to achieve an acceptable balance for the individual teacher is not easy. As we shall see in the next chapter, this matter emerges when schools seek to devise mechanisms for identifying training needs.

Much of what is contained in the previous paragraphs has a bearing on the level of learning at which INSET activities may be pitched. Breadth and depth are central concepts in this. There are times when teachers require a superficial understanding of aspects of their professional work. Thus a teacher in a secondary school who spends most of his or her time teaching GCSE classes may be marginally interested in the transfer of pupils from primary feeder schools to a secondary school, or a teacher of 11–13-year-olds may express only a passing interest in TVEI. As teachers in the school community they may require some INSET that is essentially shallow and superficial in character. For other teachers, more directly concerned with these matters, there is a need for INSET that is deeper and more thorough. For INSET providers these concepts of breadth and depth are extremely important since they colour all aspects of any provision. They determine the aims, objectives, content and teaching and learning strategies of any INSET activity.

In selecting the appropriate strategies to provide INSET in a school, the person or persons responsible must, in addition to the annual cycle of funding and INSET priorities defined in a number of ways, take into account the rich and varied repertoire of activities from which to choose. This richness has been well

SCHOOL YEAR	MATHEMATICS SCIENCE	DESIGN AND TECHNOLOGY	ENGLISH	(Provisional) GEOGRAPHY HISTORY	(Provisional) MODERN LANGUAGES MUSIC ART PHYSICAL EDUCATION
Autumn 1989	KS1-AT/PoS KS3-AT/PoS		KS1-AT/PoS		
Summer 1990					
Autumn 1990	KS2-AT/PoS	KS1-AT/PoS KS2-AT/PoS KS3-AT/PoS	KS2-AT/PoS KS3-AT/PoS		
Summer 1991	KS1-SAT[1]		KS1-SAT[1]		
Autumn 1991				KS1-AT/PoS KS2-AT/PoS KS3-AT/PoS	
Summer 1992	KS1-SAT[2] KS3-SAT[1]	KS1-SAT[1]	KS1-SAT[2]		
Autumn 1992	KS4-AT/PoS		KS4-AT/PoS		KS1-AT/PoS KS2-AT/PoS KS3-AT/PoS
Summer 1993	KS3-SAT[2]	KS1-SAT[2] KS3-SAT[1]	KS3-SAT[1]	KS1-SAT[1]	

Figure 3.3   Stages in the introduction of the National Curriculum in England.

Term					
Autumn 1993		KS4-AT/PoS			
Summer 1994	KS2-SAT[1] KS4-GCSE/SAT	KS2-SAT[1] KS3-SAT[2]	KS2-SAT[1] KS3-SAT[2] KS4-GCSE/SAT	KS1-SAT[2] KS3-SAT[1]	KS1-SAT[1]
Autumn 1994				KS4-AT/PoS	
Summer 1995	KS2-SAT[2]	KS2-SAT[2] KS4-GCSE/SAT	KS2-SAT[2]	KS2-SAT[1] KS3-SAT[2]	KS1-SAT[2] KS3-SAT[1]
Autumn 1995					KS4-AT/PoS
Summer 1996				KS2-SAT[2] KS4-GCSE/SAT	KS2-SAT[1] KS3-SAT[2]
Autumn 1996					
Summer 1997					KS2-SAT[2] KS4-GCSE/SAT

KS = Key stage
AT/PoS = Statutory attainment targets and programmes of study take effect in the first year of the key stage shown
SAT[1] = Unreported assessment
SAT[2] = First reported assessment

57

illustrated in a list compiled by Oldroyd *et al.* (1984) as part of a Schools Council programme:

A. Activities for groups in a school
1. Staff induction programmes.
2. Visits to other schools.
3. Links with feeder schools.
4. Developing tutor skills.
5. Job enrichment and rotation of tasks.
6. Team review.
7. Using management meetings for INSET.
8. Using external course activities for school-based INSET.
9. Staff development for senior management.
10. Inter-school INSET activities.

B. Interest group activities
1. Staff study groups and seminars.
2. School-based courses.
3. Self-regulating staff development.
4. Becoming a pupil for the day.
5. Co-operative teaching.
6. School-based remedial INSET group.
7. Using broadsheets.
8. Exchange of teachers.
9. Mutual lesson observation.

Some of these strategies will be discussed in later chapters. For the moment the list serves as an important contextual factor to keep in mind as consideration is given to the structural arrangements made within schools for facilitating the introduction of the various strategies.

Structural arrangements for INSET in schools

There is an integral relationship between the structure, processes and persons that constitute the elements in a school's INSET arrangements. The structure can most easily be described in terms of the formal hierarchy of teachers and functional groups adopted by any school. Schools share the same basic processes in

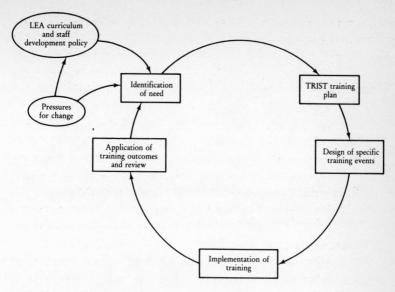

Figure 3.4   The TRIST cycle.

INSET provision (illustrated in Figure 3.4) that became familiar to schools at the time of TRIST.

This cycle emphasizes the continuity between the five stages in INSET planning and the fact that once a cycle is complete it recommences. With regard to persons, as school-based INSET has become more popular, schools have needed to find ways of ensuring that persons take on responsibility for the co-ordination of their programmes. This has tended to focus on the role of an individual who, in different schools, may be titled the staff development co-ordinator, the INSET co-ordinator, the staff development tutor, or some such title. In order to illustrate the arrangements made in some schools, some examples are quoted. In them there is an emphasis on structural arrangements and I shall describe these first before turning to look more closely at the role of INSET development co-ordinators.

Example 1

The school in this example is an 11–16 co-educational

comprehensive school with approximately 800 pupils and 46 full-time teachers. The appointment of a new headteacher in 1986 gave the school the opportunity to develop a new structure for professional development. Central to this was the designation of a deputy head as INSET Co-ordinator and the setting up of a Professional Development Committee.

One of the first tasks of the Professional Development Committee was the drafting of a formal written staff development policy. This emphasizes that account must be taken of the school as a whole, groups of staff within the school and individual members of staff in the light of improving the quality of educational provision for the pupils. There is an indication of the short term and long term targets for the school. These resulted from a staff survey and discussions both within the school at senior management level and outside the school with senior representatives of the LEA.

All the teachers in the school had completed a questionnaire in which they listed their qualifications, their INSET experiences, and their extra-curricular interests. In addition, each member of staff had an annual staff development interview with the headteacher. A further questionnaire was used to identify the teachers' training needs. This took the form of a list of INSET topics and teachers were requested to indicate their needs under three headings: relevance to the whole school, to a subject department and to the individual. In addition they were asked to list six INSET topics that they considered to be priorities for the school. The priorities thus identified were discussed in the Professional Development Committee and recommendations were made to the management and policy group, who came to decisions in the light of a staff development programme that had been designed for a three-year development period. This development programme had received the formal support of both the senior management team and a full staff meeting. For 1987–88 the following priorities were identified: cross-curricular projects, computer awareness, GCSE training, active learning methods, general management skills, school evaluation, and preparation for TVEI.

1986–87	1987–88	1988–89
1st and 2nd year craft development	1st and 2nd year craft evaluation	
1st and 2nd year microelectronics introduction	Microelectronics continuation	Microelectronics evaluation
Information technology introduction	Information technology continuation	Information technology evaluation
Multi-cultural education planning	Multi-cultural education planning	Multi-cultural education introduction
GCSE examinations continuing	GCSE examinations continuing	GCSE examinations, discussion of implications years 1–3
Business studies feasibility study	Business studies possible start	Business studies possible continuation
Alternative curriculum evaluation		
	English across the curriculum working party	English across the curriculum planning
	TVEI planning	TVEI introduction

Table 3.1 A three-year programme of curriculum planning

It is worth noting how difficult it has been for schools to plan their own INSET programmes on anything other than a one-year cycle. To some extent this reflects the annual cycle of GRIST and LEATGS funding, but it also reflects the speed of change within the education system. This can be illustrated by a three-year curriculum programme drawn up in a comprehensive school in 1986 for the years 1986–89. Table 3.1 indicates the attention paid to feasibility studies, continuation work and evaluation. The allocation of funds for INSET was to be closely tied to this programme. What is striking about the programme is the assumption that was made for 1988–89. These curriculum planners had not anticipated the proposals made for the National Curriculum, which were first discussed as part of a consultation process in 1987 and then became law with the passing of the Education Reform Act in 1988. The implementation of the curriculum proposals commenced in the autumn of 1989, which would have radically altered the sequence of planning in this and every other state school.

Returning to the earlier example, the school professional development committee, having identified its major INSET priorities, produced an INSET development plan which was presented to the whole staff and to the school governors. This plan gave details of the identified training needs, the methods of identification, the target groups for INSET, the distinction between school-based and authority-based INSET, the planned provision and the timescale for implementing the plans. The plan also included the arrangements for monitoring and evaluating INSET. All teachers who had undergone training were expected to complete a form that requested comments on the effectiveness of the training. This report could be disseminated to other teachers as appropriate. Furthermore, members of the LEA advisory staff were kept informed about the implementation of the school's plans.

Example 2

The school in this example is a co-educational 11–18 comprehensive school with some 800 pupils and 65 teachers. In response to an LEA request the senior management team in the school drew up an INSET plan for the financial year 1987–88. They attempted to produce a coherent plan that drew together separate but related programmes focusing on the whole staff, staff teams of approximately six teachers and individual teachers. This plan was based on a number of principles. The whole programme was aimed at improving the quality of learning for pupils, with principal focus on cross-curricular matters. INSET needs related to specialist subjects and to the introduction of GCSE were to be provided for on an authority-wide basis and therefore were not required in the plan. There was a developmental sequence, which commenced with changing teacher attitudes, proceeded to changing teaching and learning strategies, and concluded with changing the character of the school. The INSET programme was to be based upon a co-operative staff approach to what were judged to be relevant issues and to co-operative problem-solving, which was intended to ensure institutional momentum. INSET funding was to be allocated to activities that were cost-effective, including residential weekends, teacher release from teaching commitments and in-school secondment.

The translation of the plan into training activities was the responsibility of a member of the senior management team, who had been given a title to identify him as being specifically responsible for INSET. He devised the training programme in consultation with heads of subject departments. This programme had three parts. The first part related to the whole staff. Two days were put aside for an INSET training event for all the teachers, focusing on information technology. To extend the work accomplished in the two days a cross-faculty team was set up. This team was included in the second part of the programme in which were identified nine topics; for each topic a developmental team was established. The topics were: curriculum liaison with primary schools, information technology across the curriculum, group work, research into classroom effectiveness, records of pupil achievement/profiling, vocational and pre-vocational education, resource-based and skill-based learning, pastoral curriculum, and development of new curricula for the sixth form.

With regard to the training needs of individual teachers, 35 requests were made. The bulk of these needs would be met on an authority-wide basis and thus did not represent a charge on the school's internal INSET funds.

In this school relatively little attention had been paid to

monitoring and evaluating aspects of the INSET programme. Some members of staff who had engaged in training activities outside the school prepared written reports about them. Some of the developmental teams inside the school also produced reports for distribution to other teachers in the school. Closer attention was paid to the evaluation of the whole-school INSET days, after which teachers were expected to complete questionnaires that were read by the senior member of staff responsible for INSET.

A clear distinction was made between staff development and INSET. The staff development programme hinged upon a personal interview which each teacher had annually with the head of faculty, the head of year and, if required, a member of the senior management team. In addition to these annual reviews there were termly reviews of faculties. These staff development reviews followed specific, agreed guidelines and focused on the strengths and needs of individuals. The training needs identified in the interviews were fed into the school's INSET needs identification exercise.

In these two examples some of the major structural characteristics of school-based INSET can be detected. In both cases a senior member of staff had been given responsibility for managing the school's INSET programme. There was also teacher involvement in management committees that were responsible for identifying and prioritizing training needs and for devising an annual training programme. These planning processes were described in both schools as consultative activities involving individual teachers, departments and faculties. The school's INSET plans took account of the needs of the whole school, functional groups and individual teachers. In both schools some attention had been paid to monitoring and evaluating training experiences although these aspects of the programmes were relatively less developed in 1987–88 than other aspects. It is important to notice the distinction made in the second example between staff development and INSET. Staff development was defined in this school as teacher appraisal, a concept that has become highly contentious in recent years.

Teachers have become suspicious of central government proposals to introduce schemes of teacher appraisal into schools, since they see them as a means of weeding out those teachers who are judged to be less competent and they also see them as being used to determine the allocation of merit payments. There is clearly a grey area between a needs identification exercise and a teacher appraisal exercise, although the former has not generally been seen by teachers as contentious. Bunnell (1989) has edited a useful series of papers on teacher appraisal.

Example 3
The third example is taken from a primary school that has four full-time teachers, two part-time teachers and a head. Because of the small number of teachers each member of staff carries responsibility for more than one area of the school's work. The deputy has responsibility for mathematics, science and boys' games, another teacher has responsibility for language, a third oversees infant development and the fourth covers home–school liaison. One of the part-time teachers is responsible for audio-visual and other resources and another is responsible for girls' games. The head takes a particular interest in pupils with special needs.

The head had been recently appointed and soon after taking up her post she decided to replace the informal arrangements made for managing the school with more formal arrangements. This was reflected in the allocation of responsibilities to individual teachers and in the introduction of formal staff meetings. With regard to INSET, she tried formal interviews with each teacher as a means of reviewing the previous year's INSET activities but she found these unsatisfactory, partly because she felt that she had not prepared for them properly and partly because staff were suspicious of her motives.

A series of three staff meetings was held in a short period of time to discuss various aspects of the work of the school and at each of these meetings teachers were encouraged to give oral reports about INSET activities in which they had been engaged.

After the third of these meetings the head distributed a short questionnaire, which asked the teachers to indicate three curriculum areas in which they felt they had achieved success in the previous school year, to state the curriculum areas in which they had been less successful, to indicate the extent to which their training needs had been met and to state the kinds of INSET activities in which they wished to participate in the future. On the basis of the responses the headteacher prepared a development plan, which turned out to be too tightly tied to the school's curriculum needs as perceived by the headteacher. As the plan was being implemented, individual teachers expressed an interest in attending INSET activities that met their personal needs. Since all of the school's INSET funds had been allocated according to the headteacher's plan it was extremely difficult to cover for staff absence and so the needs of individual teachers went largely unmet. In order to take more fully into account the needs of individuals, the headteacher designed a fuller questionnaire and then prepared a development plan that sought to balance the needs of the school and the individual teachers, and also took into account the pressure from the LEA to impose upon the school ESG (Education Support Grant) projects in science and mathematics as part of their rolling programme. The evolution of this school's INSET structure and policy-making is illustrated in Figure 3.5.

Example 4
Whereas the primary school described above had a full-time staff of four teachers plus the headteacher, in this example there are ten full-time teachers plus a headteacher. This is a large primary school without an infants department. Among the ten teachers there are probationers and redeployed teachers who have undergone conversion training from secondary to primary education. Responsibility for various curriculum areas is shared between five teachers, the headteacher and the deputy head. There are seven areas of responsibility shared out between these teachers, who are described as curriculum co-ordinators: art and display, language development, mathematics, music, physical

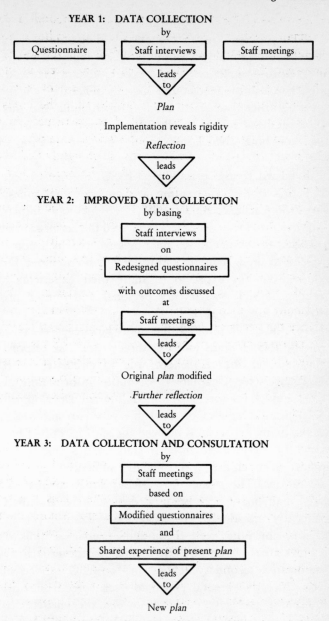

Figure 3.5   Identification of INSET needs in Brownlands School.

education, religious education and science. As in all primary schools the problem for the teachers is finding time to carry out their whole-school responsibilities when most of them are committed to a single class. The exceptions are the head and deputy. The deputy spends three-quarters of her time engaged in supporting other teachers through team teaching and this has enabled the headteacher to allot some time to the curriculum leaders for both INSET in school time and helping other teachers.

With regard to the planning of INSET in the school, the introduction of GRIST funding was an important milestone. Before 1986 teachers attended INSET activities in an unplanned and unstructured way. Teachers requested the permission of the headteacher to attend courses and other events. The headteacher responded to these requests and teachers who attended INSET activities were not expected to share their experience with colleagues. INSET was a very personal and almost private activity.

In 1987 the LEA requested all primary headteachers in its area to provide INSET plans to cover three years. The response of the headteacher in this school was to circulate a GRIDS questionnaire (see Chapter 4 for more information about GRIDS: Guidelines for Review and Internal Development in Schools) and the replies were the subject for two staff meetings. From the many expressions of need the staff identified two on which they decided to focus: mathematics and religious education. The choice was strongly influenced by external considerations. The school was already involved in an LEA-initiated mathematics project funded by an ESG and the LEA had recently introduced a new agreed syllabus for religious education, which they were encouraging primary schools to try. Two other areas were to be given some attention: liaison with the associated secondary school and an ESG funded oracy project. Once this general plan had been agreed there was a second phase (see Figure 3.6) in which the curriculum co-ordinators consulted teachers about their perceived training needs in the context of particular areas. This process of consultation provided the detailed information necessary to decide how much expertise was already located within the school that could be called upon for school-provided INSET, and how much external assistance was required. As can be seen in Figure 3.6, the result was a programme of INSET that incorporated staff visits to other schools, a consultancy role inside the school for curriculum co-ordinators, attendance of teachers at training events and the planning of whole-school staff development days. In a relatively short period of time this school had been able to effect a change from an unstructured and unplanned INSET provision for teachers as individuals to a structured and planned provision that had been agreed by the whole staff and took account of the needs of individuals, curriculum areas and the whole school.

These examples taken from two contrasting primary schools illustrate some of the ways primary schools have adapted to the changed context of INSET afforded by GRIST. Some LEAs made available fixed sums for schools to spend on INSET activities determined by their prioritization of identified needs. Some other LEAs allocated an allowance of staff to provide some cover for teachers who wished to engage in INSET related activities – planning, course attendance, experimentation with innovations, school visits, meetings with consultants, evaluation activities – during school time. Access to INSET funds and other resources required headteachers to devise appropriate arrangements for consultation and planning to occur, and in these two examples we can see headteachers taking the opportunity to move to a collegial style of management, in which teachers were active participants. As in secondary schools, we can detect the interaction between curriculum planning and management, staff development, resources management and INSET planning. However, unlike secondary schools, primary schools have relatively simple management hierarchies, although in the second primary school example there is a ladder that climbs from the probationary teacher to the curriculum co-ordinator to the deputy headteacher to the

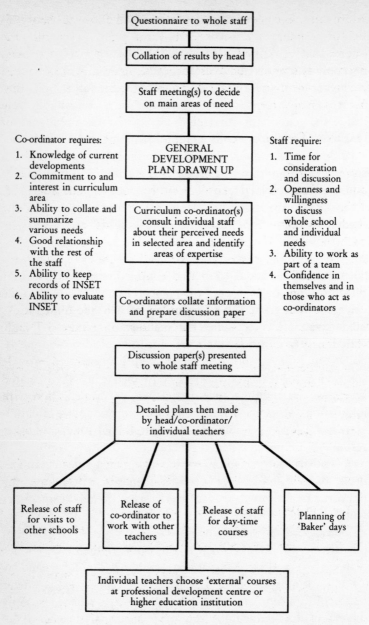

Co-ordinator requires:

1. Knowledge of current developments
2. Commitment to and interest in curriculum area
3. Ability to collate and summarize various needs
4. Good relationship with the rest of the staff
5. Ability to keep records of INSET
6. Ability to evaluate INSET

Staff require:

1. Time for consideration and discussion
2. Openness and willingness to discuss whole school and individual needs
3. Ability to work as part of a team
4. Confidence in themselves and in those who act as co-ordinators

Questionnaire to whole staff

Collation of results by head

Staff meeting(s) to decide on main areas of need

GENERAL DEVELOPMENT PLAN DRAWN UP

Curriculum co-ordinator(s) consult individual staff about their perceived needs in selected area and identify areas of expertise

Co-ordinators collate information and prepare discussion paper

Discussion paper(s) presented to whole staff meeting

Detailed plans then made by head/co-ordinator/ individual teachers

Release of staff for visits to other schools

Release of co-ordinator to work with other teachers

Release of staff for day-time courses

Planning of 'Baker' days

Individual teachers choose 'external' courses at professional development centre or higher education institution

Figure 3.6   Identification of INSET needs in Redlands School.

headteacher. In this respect there is a marked difference between the two primary schools described. In primary schools the headteacher fulfils the key role of INSET co-ordinator, whereas in secondary schools this is a role that has usually been allocated to a senior member of staff other than the head. It is to this role that we can now turn.

The INSET co-ordinator in secondary schools

A useful starting point in discussing the role of the INSET co-ordinator in secondary schools is a publication produced as part of the TRIST dissemination exercise (Bell and Rice, undated), which drew on the experience of a number of secondary schools in Cheshire and Oldham. Both LEAs had encouraged schools to nominate a person responsible for INSET. Cheshire employed the title INSET Co-ordinator and Oldham preferred the title Staff Development Tutor.

Bell and Rice identified the eight key roles of the INSET Co-ordinator/Staff Development Tutor shown in Figure 3.7 and offered these working definitions:

> The Staff Development Tutor (SDT), in seeking to *identify needs* will use many strategies including listening to colleagues, guiding them, and sometimes offering advice. These strategies, all of which have their place, are often incorrectly summarized as being those used in counselling. The *counsellor* has a much more sensitive role, which is crucial to the success of the SDT . . . .
>
> A *facilitator* by using available strategies, and acting at different levels, both internally and externally, will seek to enable developments to occur.
>
> The Staff Development Tutor, when organising and managing the process of change is acting in the role of *administrator*. This will involve the oversight and handling of detailed tasks such as correspondence and record keeping.
>
> An *innovator* will be well informed both of internal developments and of external priorities and will draw upon his or her own expertise and that of others. He or she will act as a change agent and will present ideas or developments clearly and objectively as well as being sensitive to the timing of change.

71

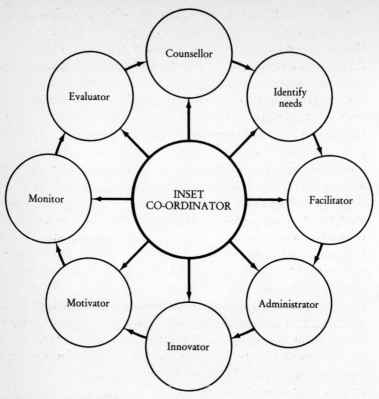

Figure 3.7   Key roles.

By his or her own example, the Staff Development Tutor as *motivator* will seek to engender enthusiasm in colleagues as well as maintain momentum and morale.

In the role of *monitor,* the SDT will maintain a watching brief, gathering evidence, which will be used to evaluate.

To assess the effectiveness of the present situation or of innovations undertaken, it will be necessary to bring judgement to bear on the evidence gathered during the monitoring process. The Staff Development Tutor is acting in the role of *evaluator*. Evaluation may indicate the successful implementation of the development undertaken. Where this has not occurred, evaluation will lead to the identification of new needs. (p. 9)

This is a useful list that provides secondary schools with an ideal target at which to aim. However, the appointment of INSET co-ordinators has been accomplished with varying degrees of success, depending on the particular circumstances of individual schools. Much depends on identifying a member of staff at senior level who is not already heavily over-burdened with other responsibilities and who has the necessary interest, enthusiasm and competence, together with the respect and trust of colleagues, to take on the role. An inquiry conducted on the role of INSET co-ordinators in one LEA revealed some of the difficulties they met in the schools.

In the metropolitan LEA chosen for the study there were thirteen secondary schools and one sixth form college. Each school had nominated a Staff Development Co-ordinator (SDC) and eleven of the fourteen were deputy heads. For the majority of them the role of SDC had been bolted onto existing responsibilities. As part of their induction into their new roles they had attended a residential conference, which focused on a number of issues, including job analysis, designing a staff development system, needs identification exercises, developing a whole-school approach to INSET, staff development interviewing, networking, implementing change and the development of strategies for action. The SDCs, most of whom had been TRIST co-ordinators from 1985 to 1987, took on their new roles in 1987. Interviews conducted with each of them indicated that in the first year their principal function had been to locate appropriate courses offered outside the school for teachers who expressed an interest in obtaining some form of INSET. The SDCs experienced some difficulty in finding the time to carry out this relatively straightforward task. Most of them had teaching timetables that took up, on average, approximately 45 per cent of their school time. In the rest of their time they had to fulfil a number of responsibilities in addition to their INSET role.

Part of their work was defined by requirements made by the LEA. In 1986 each school had been asked to identify five priority INSET needs. In 1987, in addition to a request for

73

identified needs, they were asked to provide the names of teachers who were interested in the award of teaching fellowships by the LEA and to identify the areas of staff expertise that teachers could offer.

In this identification of training needs these co-ordinators initially relied largely upon informal methods. They responded to requests from individual teachers. Conversations with colleagues appeared to predominate. In 1987 only two SDCs had set up a co-ordinating committee, six had introduced a training needs questionnaire and four had used formal interviews with teachers. The needs identified by individual schools had been communicated to the LEA and used to determine the LEA's local INSET priorities. These, in 1987, were: school management, the personal and social development of pupils, TVEI related INSET, curriculum development, teaching skills and learning strategies, and community education.

In this early stage of accommodating to GRIST funding, INSET was provided largely in the shape of courses run by the LEA and other providers outside the school. INSET was synonymous with course attendance. However, there was a shift towards more school-focused activities and within a year all but two of the SDCs had contacted providers external to the LEA in order to discuss in-school provision of INSET. The training events organized inside the schools focused on such topics as computer literacy, computer awareness, probationer induction, pupil profiling, and personal and social education. The introduction of compulsory staff development days provided a fillip for school-based INSET. Interestingly, in the first year in which six staff development days became part of the school programme the majority of schools had the content of the days determined either by the heads acting alone or by the schools' senior management teams. In only one school was it reported that the staff had been consulted about the use to be made of the days.

With regard to the monitoring of INSET, the SDCs reported that this largely took the form of returning information requested by the LEA for its own monitoring purposes. This information provided a record of teacher participation and did not include any monitoring of the quality and effectiveness of any INSET undertaken. No attempts were made to cascade the experiences through subject departments, faculties or the whole school. There was no requirement for teachers to produce any kind of report of what they had learned from attendance at any training activity. The SDCs had received no requirement from the LEA to initiate any INSET evaluation in their schools and there was no evidence of any formal evaluation taking place.

As the SDCs learned and developed their new roles they identified changes which they anticipated being introduced in their schools. These are shown in Table 3.2, where there is evidence of an increased formalization of the INSET role. Importance is attached to a more consultative and collegial approach and this finds expression in the establishment of a staff development committee within the school's organization structure. The need for a formal staff development interview and the establishment of effective monitoring and evaluation arrangements are also evident. In 1987–88 these SDCs had some considerable way to go before they could match the 37 criteria of effectiveness that O'Sullivan *et al.* (1988) listed for SDCs.

	Number of schools
1. Staff development committee	9
2. Professional interview	8
3. Formal monitoring	7
4. Formal evaluation	4
5. Needs questionnaire	3
6. Other needs identification	2
7. GRIDS	1

Table 3.2 Anticipated changes in INSET processes.

In their report on the implementation of the first year of LEATGS, HMI (1989b) stated that of the 68 LEAs they had visited, 60 had devolved INSET funds to their schools. It was this funding, together with the introduction of the six staff development days, that had accelerated the attention paid to school-based INSET. However, HMI also emphasized that the sums devolved were often very small relative to the costs of provision. They reported that insufficient attention had been paid in LEAs to the training of those persons in school who carried the responsibility for the management and organization of school-based INSET. These persons were hampered by the administrative burden of form-filling that accompanied delegated budgets. Finally, matching need to provision proved difficult, especially when the co-ordinators received information about INSET provision too late for their planning cycle.

Review

What emerges from this chapter is that INSET planning and implementation in schools were stimulated by the introduction of TRIST funding. The requirement that close attention should be paid to the formal organization and management of INSET saw the introduction of TRIST co-ordinators in many second-ary schools. The introduction of LEATGS reinforced this development and it was extended into all schools, including primary schools. Devolved INSET budgets, although small in size, alerted schools to the possibility of providing INSET on their own sites. The one-year cycle of funding demanded a tight planning procedure, which included needs identification, prioritization of needs, the matching of school needs with LEA plans and national priorities, the striking of a balance between the needs of individual teachers, functional groups and the whole school, and appropriate monitoring and evaluation arrangements. Overshadowing this activity were the new conditions of service imposed upon teachers and the government proposals for teacher appraisal. More recently, there has been a massive intervention in schools' developing work in INSET following the passing of the Education Reform Act. This has led to priority being given to an agenda for INSET that has been set by central government, and LEAs have had to adjust their planning and implementation arrangements for INSET to the timescale demanded for the introduction of the National Curriculum and the school management proposals contained in the Act.

Schools have been seeking to achieve appropriate structural arrangements that locate INSET into their other organizational aspects. They have been seeking to establish linkages between INSET development, curriculum development, resources management and staff development. The structural response has been the identification of a senior member of staff with the responsibility to co-ordinate INSET, a multi-faceted task that is very burdensome, and the creation of INSET committees to represent the interests of individuals and functional groups in schools. The processes for planning and implementing INSET were clearly laid out for secondary schools through the TRIST programme, and the TRIST cycle of stages, from needs identification through planning and implementation to evaluation, has become familiar in all primary and secondary schools. We can now take a closer look at some of these processes.

4 Identifying training needs

As we have seen, the identification of training needs is the key to the INSET planning process. ACSET (1984) had attempted to identify conditions for the effectiveness of INSET and offered the following list:

1. Identification by teachers of their training needs in relation to the objectives of the school and the LEA, and to their own professional development.
2. Support of governors, the headteacher and senior staff and local authority advisers and involvement of the whole staff.
3. A coherent LEA policy (which should include helping schools and colleges to develop coherent INSET policies).
4. Precise 'targeting' of provision.
5. Choice of the appropriate form of INSET, whether individual to the teacher, school-based or externally based.
6. Choice of appropriate length of course and mode of activity.
7. Relevance to the teachers' needs and focused on practice.
8. Appropriate expertise on the part of higher education institutions and other providers of INSET.
9. Appropriate preparatory and follow-up work in schools.

The authors of the ACSET report owed much to the document *Making INSET Work*, produced by their predecessor, ACSTT, in 1978. Here a distinction was made between those teachers' training needs of a concrete and immediate kind, stemming from the teacher's everyday experience in classroom and school, and those career-related and professional needs that varied from teacher to teacher according to circumstances. To assist teachers in coming to terms with need identification a number of questions were posed:

How can you and your colleagues define the distinctive needs of particular groups: departments, year groups, those at different levels of responsibility, those charged with carrying through a particular innovation, those about to change their role?

How often should you and your colleagues review your needs and how can this best be done?

Can you review your own needs unassisted? What advice or guidelines would be helpful?

How can your head best fulfil the responsibility for identifying and meeting the needs of the school and the staff development needs of you and your colleagues?

How open should be the appraisal of needs in your school?

Are the review arrangements likely to be the same if the possibility of promotion is involved?

In a series of meetings held under the auspices of TRIST (North West), and attended by senior advisers drawn from fifteen LEAs, attention was focused on methods being used to identify training needs. In our published report of these meetings we distinguished between two models currently in use: the qualitative and the quantitative (Williams and England 1986).

The survey model: quantitative data

In this model the LEA and/or the school design their own questionnaires or adopt questionnaires produced by external agencies and use them to ask heads and teachers to relate INSET needs to the school's curriculum and management policies. Using this method, assuming the co-operation of the persons receiving the questionnaire, the total INSET needs of a school or an LEA can be speedily quantified. From the data, decision-makers in the LEA and the school can devise a training plan, which should attempt to meet immediate, intermediate and long term needs. It should also take into account national, LEA, school and teacher priorities. The key to the model is the nomination of a person at a senior level in the LEA and the school to process the accumulated data in such a way that expressed needs are placed in an order of priority. A sensitive treatment of the expressed needs is required so that the eventual match between needs and provision can be seen and understood by the teachers.

What the model takes into account can be expressed in a diagram. In Figure 4.1 the urgency factor, priorities and levels of need are the three dimensions illustrated. Each dimension has three components and in Table 4.1 the levels of need have been further refined to illustrate how complicated the dimensions become.

LEAs in the series of TRIST meetings expressed a number of difficulties in using quantitative methods to identify needs:

> Some teachers are wary of identifying and expressing their needs since they regard needs identification as a back door method of staff appraisal.

> There is a great diversity in the ability of senior staff in schools to consult with their teachers in order to produce schools' INSET needs and policies. Evidence from LEAs indicated that some schools made no

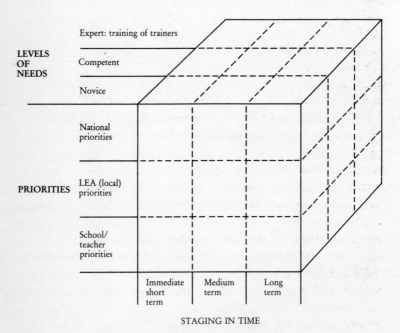

Figure 4.1   Dimensions of INSET needs identification.
Source: Williams *et al.* (1988)

Levels of need	INSET tasks
Level one: novice Newcomer to the selected topic	Arouse interest Provide introductory information Examine attitudes Diagnose levels of competence and establish foundations for further development
Level two: competent Adequate understanding and competence to cope	Maintain interest Extend knowledge and understanding Modify attitudes Assess levels of competence and extend competence
Level three: very competent High level of understanding	Training of trainers Enrich knowledge and understanding Improve competence

Table 4.1 Levels of need and relevant INSET tasks

returns and in others heads failed to develop a system which nudges the school INSET co-ordinators towards the LEA's desired mode of operation.

An insensitive treatment of the data collected can produce an INSET profile which does not actually represent any particular individual's needs. Inevitably information gathered from individuals must be aggregated to provide a school profile and if these profiles are then subjected to further aggregation the overall result is to diminish the needs of individuals and departments.

Care must be taken to design appropriate questionnaires in order to elicit INSET needs and such questionnaires must take into account the levels of INSET need and the longer term career intentions of teachers. In discussion reference was made to the distinction between the immediate needs of teachers, e.g. the improvement of specified classroom management skills, and the longer term needs for those teachers with ambitions of promotion within the education service.

These concerns indicate that needs identification is not a neutral activity. It is loaded with potential difficulties, some derived from principles and others of a technical nature. The most serious difficulty is the first in the above list. Teacher appraisal has both a positive staff development side and a negative side that highlights teacher incompetence and professional deficits. This is not the place to begin a lengthy digression into the current state of the teacher appraisal debate. (Comprehensive discussion of teacher appraisal can be found in Bunnell 1989). Suffice to say that the overlap between staff development policies and INSET policies in schools is most evident in the structures established in schools to develop the policies. Both require the central involvement of senior staff, which means heads and deputies in secondary schools and heads alone in all but the larger primary schools.

There are several INSET needs identification methods available for LEAs and schools to consider and evaluate. A comprehensive review of these was undertaken by Robinson and Thompson (1987). They listed ten methods of identifying needs: brainstorming; annual review interview; professional tutor; staff training profile; questionnaires – LEA and school; GRIDS; DION; SIGMA; school self-evaluation checklists; and children's views. To this list can be added the Training and Development Needs Questionnaire produced by the National Development Centre for School Management Training (Capell *et al.* 1987; Poster *et al.* 1987).

It is not my intention to review all the items included in the list. To illustrate some of the methods currently popular in schools I have chosen to focus on GRIDS and the use of questionnaires designed by LEAs. I shall refer briefly to published questionnaires before looking in some detail at how needs identification was being developed in the primary schools in one LEA.

GRIDS

GRIDS (Guidelines for Review and Internal Development in Schools) is an acronym that has become familiar in primary and secondary schools throughout England and Wales. It is the title for a programme of work initiated by the Schools Council following a conference in 1981 on school self-evaluation. The focus of the programme was systematic self-review of policy and practice in primary and secondary schools. Although the Schools Council no longer exists, the work continues and in this the two handbooks, one for primary schools and the other for secondary schools (McMahon *et al.* 1984a, b), are essential reading.

Underpinning the process of school review advocated in GRIDS are seven key principles:

(a) The aim is to achieve internal school development and not produce a report for formal accountability purposes.

(b) The main purpose is to move beyond the review stage into development for school improvement.

(c) The staff of the school should be consulted and involved in the review and development process as much as possible.

(d) Decisions about what happens to any information or reports produced should rest with the teachers and others concerned.

(e) The head and teachers should decide whether and how to involve the other groups in the school, e.g. pupils, parents, advisers, governors.

(f) Outsiders (e.g. external consultants) should be invited to provide help and advice when this seems appropriate.

(g) The demands made on key resources like time, money and skilled personnel should be realistic and feasible for schools and LEAs (McMahon *et al.* 1984b).

The GRIDS team advocate a review process that focuses on one or two central issues in a school's curriculum or organization. The task for the school staff is to identify the issues and then follow a series of stages, each broken into steps, of systematic review. There are five stages: getting started; initial review; specific review; action for development; and overview and re-start. In the fourth stage one of the steps is the consideration of how best to meet the various needs of the teachers involved in the development. This is a clear reminder that any changes in school curriculum and organization will result in the articulation of training needs. The organization of

83

INSET is an integral part of the GRIDS process. However, the GRIDS process can be applied to improving the arrangements made in a school for staff development and INSET. How best to identify and prioritize training needs has been one of the issues highlighted in stage 3 – specific review – in some primary and secondary schools. In stage 3 the first step is to plan the specific review by clarifying the roles of the persons engaged in the review, understanding why the issue to be reviewed was selected, identifying the persons who will be most helpful in conducting the review and drawing up a review timetable. In the second step the reviewers must find out not only what the current policy for the review issue is in the school but also how the existing policy is implemented. In the third step the emphasis is upon determining how effective the policy is and this leads to the final step, which is agreeing conclusions and making recommendations. It is in this stage that any weaknesses in the arrangements for staff development and INSET will emerge and the final step is likely to contain recommendations for improvement.

The important lesson from GRIDS is that training needs can be identified as part of a consultative review process which, if all the stages and steps are followed, will lead to thorough discussion, careful documentation and deliberate attempts to change existing patterns and arrangements. The needs of the whole school, functional groups and individuals should be taken into account in this process, and these needs will be sorted and prioritized according to the sequence of issues subject to the specific reviews.

McMahon and her colleagues (1984b) write: 'School development and improvement almost invariably involve some form of in-service training for the staff . . . The development team will need to consider what type of in-service provision will be suitable, given teachers' requirements and the availability of resources.'

Certain conditions must be met in schools for GRIDS to be used successfully. The experience of the central team (McMahon *et al.* 1984b) pointed to the following factors:

- The head clearly demonstrates his/her support, e.g. by joining a specific review team.
- The momentum of the review and development exercise was sustained by the school co-ordinator and the whole process was carefully planned and monitored.
- The specific review co-ordinator had status in the organisation and the team was integrated into the existing decision-making machinery of the school.
- The specific review team selected appropriate methods of collecting and analysing data.
- The staff were informed and consulted at every stage.

Identifying INSET needs: questionnaires

In this section I shall briefly compare two published questionnaires designed to identify INSET needs, before describing a questionnaire that I helped to produce for use by secondary school INSET co-ordinators.

DION is an acronym for Diagnosing Individual and Organizational Needs and was developed by Elliott-Kemp and Williams (1979). Essentially, this is a method of reviewing the current organizational arrangements in a school. Sixty-six statements are listed and these are comments on individuals, functional groups and the school as a whole. Examples include: 'There is not enough challenge or stimulation in my work.' 'Different jobs and tasks in the school are not properly co-ordinated.' 'Innovations do not seem to have any lasting impact here.'

The lists are intended to be used by individuals, groups or all the teachers in a school. The first task is to decide whether or not each statement is true of the school. The responses to each statement are logged on a grid. When the grid has been completed a score can be calculated by adding up a final column. A computer program has been written to assist in the process of collation. Constructing the grid serves as a stimulus for the respondent. As in GRIDS, it marks the first step in a process of school self-evaluation and review. It assists in focusing attention on particular facets of school life, so enabling an action plan to be devised that rests on a staff consultative process. Clearly, it is possible for teachers to devise their own lists of statements and this is not an uncommon experience in discussion sessions in INSET meetings and management meetings in schools. Ideas, or statements, may be listed as part of an agenda or they may be generated in discussions where the conclusions are written on flip charts for consideration by others. With the process of considering the current state of particular aspects of school life complete, the design and implementation of a plan will highlight those aspects that cannot be achieved without in-service training for individuals and groups within the school.

The National Development Centre for School Management Training collaborated with Dudley LEA to produce the Training and Development Needs Questionnaire, which has sufficient flexibility for it to be used by LEAs, by schools or by individual teachers. On a single page, biographical information for an individual teacher in either a primary or a secondary school can be recorded and then needs can be indicated from a long list of items. The items are divided into four categories: curriculum (25 items), pupils (six items), external links (eight items) and management (eight items). For each item it is possible for a teacher to record an order of priority (highest priority, fairly high priority and low priority) and select a preferred method of training or development from six choices: school-based activity, external short course/workshop, visits to other schools, secondment to another job/institution, extended long course in own time, extended long course full-time or part-time, and other.

The authors of the questionnaire emphasize that 'The use of a questionnaire to assess INSET needs is plainly only one method available to LEAs. Its principal merit is that it can give direct access to the teaching force. It must not be seen in isolation but as one method among a number of useful and well tried alternatives' (Capell *et al.* 1987). The principal purposes of the questionnaire, which is produced as three copies on sensitized paper, are stated by the authors as:

- To provide the LEA with statistical evidence of their teachers' self-identified INSET needs.
- To provide a direct link between the LEA and its teaching staff in determining INSET needs.
- To raise awareness about the INSET needs of teachers.
- To assist in determining the INSET needs of groups of schools, an individual school, departments or groups within a school, and individual staff.
- To enable a comparison to be made between the perceived needs of the LEA, the school and the individual in order to match provision with need.
- To supply evidence of INSET needs to the providers in higher and further education.
- To stimulate and support dialogue and discussion regarding INSET at all levels within the LEA.

The questionnaire is designed to enable easy preparation of the data for computer analysis. Programs are available for mainframe and microcomputers and these enable the following information to be provided: a summary or count of the information contained in the questionnaires; a summary of information for selected groups, e.g. teachers by phase or by specialist subject; a list of teachers seeking training in a particular topic; a list of topics in priority order for training and development.

Both DION and the NDC/Dudley questionnaire aim to provide a quick and comprehensive way of gathering information from individual teachers, groups of teachers and whole schools. The importance of speed needs to be emphasized given the short periods available for planning and providing INSET activities. In both cases questionnaires are not stand-alone instruments. There is a need for them to be seen as complements to discussion in such contexts as staff meetings, in-house conferences and training workshops, and also to the counselling of individual teachers by INSET co-ordinators, senior staff in schools and LEA staff. It is important for the results of the questionnaire analysis to be made available to every teacher who completed one.

While these questionnaires were intended to have general applicability, other questionnaires have been produced by individual schools or LEAs. Figure 4.2 reproduces the top page of a six-page questionnaire that was designed for use by secondary school INSET co-ordinators in a particular LEA. This follows closely the dimensions illustrated in Figure 4.1. On the left hand side are listed topics categorized by statements of national priority (as in DES LEATGS Circulars), LEA priorities (as in submissions made annually by the LEA to the DES for INSET funding) and school priorities (decided in whole-school consultation procedures). The national priorities listed in the extract are those for the year 1987–88. For each topic a teacher is requested to indicate four things: the level of importance he or she attaches to the topic; the level of urgency for training; his or her level of competence; and the preferred mode of delivery for the training. It was intended that this questionnaire would be useful to a busy secondary school INSET co-ordinator in gathering information personal to each teacher but also in indicating patterns of urgency and preferred delivery, which would assist in the planning of a school's INSET programme. The columns on levels of trainee competence would also identify those teachers who could be used as trainers within the schools for particular topics.

The questionnaires described all serve the valuable purpose of focusing the attention of teachers precisely on their own needs, which have to be put alongside whole-school, LEA and national priorities. For the senior staff who are responsible for gathering the information and collating the results the questionnaires need to be put alongside other information gathered informally and formally by other means. Much depends on the ethos and morale within the individual schools. What is important is that policy and practice for INSET can be seen to be closely associated with the needs identification procedures. Teachers are soon disillusioned by the filling of forms that appear to be ignored as soon as they have been collected.

IDENTIFICATION OF INSET NEEDS INFORMATION	LEVEL OF IMPORTANCE			LEVEL OF URGENCY			LEVEL OF TRAINEE COMPETENCE			PREFERRED DELIVERY							
NATIONAL PRIORITY AREAS	1	2	3	1	2	3	1	2	3	School-based	Course-based	Consultant	Support from school staff	Adviser-led	Distance learning pack	Reading relevant literature	Award-bearing
Management																	
Mathematics																	
Science																	
CDT																	
One year retraining – shortage subjects																	
SEN hearing																	
SEN sight																	
SEN severe learning difficulties																	
SEN designated teachers in ordinary schools																	
Industry, economy, the world of work																	
Planning school curriculum in multi-ethnic education																	
New technology across the curriculum																	
Religious education																	
Assessment of achievement																	
Drugs																	

Figure 4.2   Part of an INSET needs identification questionnaire.

The identification of INSET needs in primary schools

In the autumn of 1987 I supervised a detailed study of the arrangements made for identifying INSET needs in all 74 primary schools in a single metropolitan LEA. A questionnaire was specially designed and distributed to headteachers. Their responses indicate very clearly the pattern of approaches adopted by primary schools to identify needs. In addition, eight schools were selected for detailed study; these were visited and in-depth interviews were conducted with the headteachers. All the schools had been stimulated to undertake needs identification by the LEA, who had requested each school to prepare a three-year INSET development plan for 1987–90.

We were looking for answers to the following questions:

- What structures had been designed by headteachers to identify needs?
- What processes had been used to identify needs and which of these processes were found to be most useful?
- How much influence did groups other than the staff of the school have on the identification of needs?
- What difficulties were encountered during the process of needs identification?
- What gains were made during the process?
- What forms of help would headteachers prefer in the future identification of needs, particularly in the longer term?

Completed questionnaires, which yielded abundant information, were returned by 67 (90 per cent) of the headteachers.

Figure 4.3 illustrates the structures of responsibility for INSET needs identification designed by the headteachers. In a large proportion (48 per cent) of schools responsibility for identifying INSET needs rested with the whole staff and there was a further 9 per cent where responsibility rested with each teacher as an individual. In contrast, only four headteachers (6 per cent) had formally delegated responsibility to another teacher, only four (6 per cent) had set up a small formal group to take that responsibility, and only one headteacher had assigned responsibility to the subject co-ordinators. Perhaps

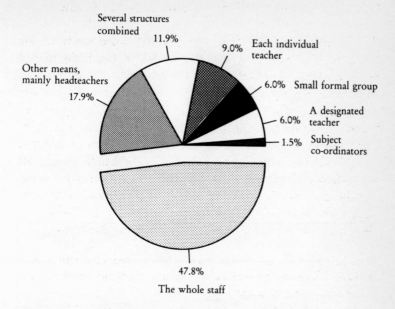

Figure 4.3   Structures of responsibility for INSET needs identification.

surprisingly, only ten headteachers (15 per cent) saw themselves as the structural focus for the identification of INSET needs.

This may be a reflection of the way in which primary school teachers generally work together as equals under the leadership of the headteacher and deputy. It may also reflect the way each class teacher is directly involved in teaching almost all areas of the curriculum. Most individual teachers, usually deputy headteachers, who have been given direct responsibility for the identification of INSET needs have several other onerous responsibilities. In only one case was the responsibility for INSET needs identification given to a teacher with no other responsibilities.

The requirement to identify INSET needs formally in primary schools was new in this LEA in 1987 and it is to be expected that subsequent practice would change in the light of experience.

Processes of identifying needs

The processes of identifying needs are listed in Table 4.2. Headteachers were asked to pick out the three processes they had found most helpful and a summary of their responses is given in Table 4.3. The processes fall fairly easily into four main areas:

1. *The whole staff.* Full staff meetings at lunchtime and after school were the most widely used process and headteachers also ranked them high in effectiveness, as can be seen in Table 4.3. This reflects and confirms the majority of the headteachers' assigning the responsibility for identification of needs to the whole staff.

	Percentage of schools ($n = 67$)
1. Staff meetings after school	78
2. Work arising from ESG projects	77
3. Work on curriculum document	72
4. Staff meetings at lunchtime	57
5. Previous INSET	45
6. Keeping written records	40
7. Consultants	37
8. School devised questions	30
9. Classroom observation	28
10. LEA self-evaluation document	28
11. Formal staff interviews	25
12. Formal contact with advisers	18
13. GRIDS	15
14. Written reports by staff	15

Table 4.2 Processes used in needs identification

	Percentage of schools ($n = 67$)
1. Staff meetings after school	30
2. Staff meetings at lunchtime	30
3. Work arising from ESG projects	28
4. Work on curriculum document	24
5. Formal staff interview	16
6. School-devised questionnaires	16
7. Consultants	8
8. Previous INSET	7
9. Classroom observation	4
10. GRIDS	4
11. Formal contact with advisers	3
12. Keeping written records	3
13. Written reports by staff	1

Table 4.3 Most helpful ways of identifying needs

2. *Support services.* After full staff meetings, work done on ESG schemes, discussions with consultants and experience arising from previous INSET activity were the main sources for needs identification. Fifty-two (77 per cent) headteachers indicated that work done under an ESG scheme had revealed INSET needs but, more significantly perhaps, nineteen (28 per cent) placed this among the most helpful. Experience of previous INSET activities was used in 30 (45 per cent) schools and was found most helpful by five headteachers. Next in impact came the work of the LEA consultants, who were cited 24 times, and were found to be most helpful in six cases.

There were only twelve headteachers (18 per cent) who indicated that formal collaboration between their staff and members of the advisory service took place in the process of identifying needs and only one of these found this formal collaboration most helpful. The influence of the advisory service may have been informal and therefore does not appear as often as it might in the responses. However, only one headteacher mentioned the school adviser as consulting with him or her over the identification of needs as an extra to the listed possibilities.

3. *Individual teachers.* In 20 (30 per cent) schools individual teachers' views were elicited by asking them to fill in questionnaires designed within their schools. In seventeen (25 per cent) schools individual teachers were interviewed formally. It is noteworthy that a large proportion of those headteachers who used these two methods found them among the most helpful processes: 59 per cent of those who used a staff questionnaire and 66 per cent of those who used a formal interview asterisked these as most helpful.

4. *Written resources.* As can be seen in Table 4.2, the main written resource used to help identify needs was the school's curriculum document. Forty-eight schools (72 per cent) used this document and sixteen headteachers found it among the most helpful. Nineteen schools (28 per cent) used their LEA document, 'Self-evaluation in primary schools', but surprisingly, perhaps, none of them indicated this as among the most useful aid in the identification of needs. Ten schools (15 per cent) used the GRIDS approach but, of these, only three found it most helpful.

Headteachers were also invited to describe any other procedures they had used in identifying needs, including informal and formal procedures. Three headteachers explained that informal consultation with individual teachers took place and one felt that this informal approach had been among the most useful means of identifying needs, while another pointed out that in a small school, with very few staff, formal meetings and interviews were not only inappropriate but also almost impossible to arrange since all, including the headteacher, were teaching almost all the time.

Another headteacher, indicating a more formal approach, listed: '(1) re-definition of posts of responsibility/areas of responsibility; (2) re-negotiation of job descriptions; (3) review of the curriculum'. Another process referred to by three headteachers was consultation with other primary schools and associated high schools: 'High school "feeders" combined to organize area INSET since 1985; school staffs were polled to identify needs.' 'There was discussion with other primary schools and the associated secondary school at headteacher level.' This last was asterisked as being among the most helpful procedures used by that school and responses to other questions suggest that several headteachers consider links with other schools to be very beneficial.

One headteacher described the INSET log used in his or her school: 'All staff enter courses attended, duration, etc. At the end of the academic year I analyse the staff hours of INSET (courses and in-house) on a subject area basis to identify neglected areas.' Such an INSET log might be very useful over a period of time and if it included existing areas of expertise, however acquired, through INSET, initial training or previous experience, it might prevent the neglect of such areas of expertise, as well as enabling gaps and shortfalls to be identified.

Outside influences on the identification of needs

A summary of the responses to the question that asked headteachers to indicate the degree of involvement in the identification of needs by listed outside groups is contained in Table 4.4. This shows the percentage of schools indicating high involvement, some involvement and little or no involvement of the various groups that were included in the questionnaire. Several headteachers felt unable to indicate the degree of involvement of some of the groups listed. These never reached more than 10 per cent for any group and are not included in the tables.

Table 4.4 shows clearly that the three most influential groups were the ESG project teams, the advisory service and other primary schools; the three least influential groups were the governors, the parents and staff from higher education. The LEA consultants and high schools had a small but noticeable contribution to make.

Headteachers were also asked to specify any other groups that had had any influence on their schools' identification of needs. A list of those outside influences is given below. The numbers in

	Percentages ($n = 67$) showing		
	High involvement	Some involvement	Little or no involvement
1. The ESG teams	45	27	22
2. Other primary schools	29	14	50
3. Advisory service	21	42	33
4. GRIST consultants	15	21	52
5. High schools	15	16	60
6. Governors	2	18	78
7. Parents	2	4	87
8. Staff from higher education	0	3	89

Table 4.4 Outside group involvement

parentheses show the number of headteachers who indicated a particular influence.

Cluster meetings with high schools and feeder primary schools (3).
HMI (4).
DES documents and important reports (3).
The pupils (4).
Former pupils (1).
Peripatetic Remedial Service (2).
Pupils in school who have special needs (2).
Non-teaching assistants (NNEB) (1).
Small schools group (1).
English Language Teaching Service (1).
Certain courses attended by individual teachers (3).

How much outside groups can and/or should be involved in the identification of needs is a question that is likely to bring forth many different opinions and the responses of the head-teachers reflect some of these differences. One headteacher asserted:

The individual teacher, if he or she is honest, knows very well what his or her needs are. Whether they choose to do something about those needs is another matter. They shouldn't need to have them identified by any other group. If they can't recognize their own needs, they shouldn't be teaching.

Another headteacher struck a warning note about the increasing pressures from outside groups:

The primary identification of INSET needs should come from within the school. The advice and support of outside groups is necessary and clearly of benefit, but I would not like to see a situation developing where such groups were dictating INSET priorities to the school. I am sure that there is a danger of this happening and I think safeguards need to be built in to prevent schools losing control of the power to decide their own INSET priorities.

Another suggested a major problem for any outside group attempting to identify needs:

The difficulty with outside groups attempting to identify rather than meet INSET needs in the school is that unless the group represented is one closely associated with the establishment, e.g. school advisers, ESG team, the approach should highlight procedures which in general were already identified by the school; to be effective the outside group really needs to know the institution before an opinion can be ventured upon anything other than standard models of INSET identification.

Yet another headteacher saw the problem from a slightly different angle:

Outside groups will exert pressure for identification of INSET needs according to how they perceive the situation. This may be generated by either national or local initiatives or for purely selfish reasons. This may be particularly true in the case of the outside group being parents. The development should take the form of a greater awareness of particular need rather than falling into the trap of sweeping generalizations.

Although several headteachers may have had reservations about outside involvement in the identification of needs, all acknowledged that outside groups do have a part to play. One expressed the balance that headteachers seem to feel should be maintained between the school-based identification of needs and the involvement of outside groups.

> I feel quite strongly that maximum freedom should be allowed for schools to identify INSET needs without external pressure. However, I feel equally strongly that a school that does not heed and indeed seek external advice when particular difficulties arise is unwise. To summarize – I feel that schools should make themselves aware of external concerns, evaluate those concerns and act accordingly.

Another reflected accurately the generally very positive tone of most of the responses:

> An input into an area of the curriculum which has hitherto been taken for granted always makes for re-thinking and a demand to be brought up-to-date. I see outside groups as stimuli to self-evaluation within the school and would like regular changes of emphasis (not every year!)

This positive stance is certainly taken by the 33 per cent of headteachers who made reference to links with other schools as an area of involvement with external groups that they already found useful and would like to develop further. These links were between groups or clusters of primary schools and between high schools and their feeder primary schools. Some of the needs mentioned as having been identified from links between high schools and primary schools had been quite specific.

> High school liaison has influenced me in identifying pupil needs in the top junior classes and thus, indirectly, influenced INSET.

> Seminars and demonstrations with 'experts' from high schools and primary schools have identified teachers' areas of weakness in Art. We feel this could be extended to other areas.

Other headteachers expressed the hope that existing practice would continue and that further progress would be made. One headteacher succinctly related this to the liaison between primary and secondary schools:

> Liaison with the local high school is progressing in all areas of the curriculum – a deeper understanding by the high school staff of the work undertaken in the 'feeder' junior schools is developing, as too is

the understanding by the staff at the feeder junior school of the work undertaken by the high schools ... Communication between secondary and junior schools could be developed with a view to co-ordinating teaching to accommodate the GCSE examination. The development of mutual support between neighbouring primary schools and the local high school ... will contribute to the delivery of a true comprehensive curriculum and precise primary/secondary links.

Several headteachers referred to the benefits already gained from working in close collaboration with other primary schools. The Small Schools Association initiated in the LEA was mentioned favourably and one headteacher commented: 'The LEA and clusters of local schools are following the right path to more INSET involvement.'

Although most references to clusters and primary school links were very positive, a warning note was sounded: 'Care must be taken that, whilst working towards common aims, the individual character and development of each school is preserved.' Emphasizing that sharing is not always possible, another headteacher asserted that: 'The involvement of other schools has proved difficult because of their different aims and we have therefore opted for "in-house" provision where possible'.

This reminder of the individuality of schools was perhaps timely when grouping was seen as so beneficial by many of the headteachers. Another slightly cautionary note was sounded by the 'necessity for a co-ordinated approach within our primary cluster' and the need to work 'towards improved inter-primary and primary/high school links in order to co-ordinate better curricular development and co-operation'. Such links and co-operative groupings clearly need not only commitment but also efficient organization.

Another source of help in identifying needs referred to by several headteachers is the LEA support services: the advisory service, the ESG teams, the LEA consultants, the English Language Teaching Service and the Peripatetic Remedial Service. These are generally seen as groups that have a real contribution to make. Their contacts with the schools were close and the persons concerned were seen as having both practical experience and theoretical knowledge. The ESG teams had been very successful in helping to identify specific needs in relation to their particular curriculum area and in almost all cases were referred to in favourable terms, but there is a difficulty inherent in the LEA ESG model. One headteacher highlighted the problem:

> We had an INSET policy which was working well. The imposition and timing of the ESG schemes interfered with rather than helped this work. It would be churlish to suggest we did not benefit from ESG because they proved most beneficial. However, the top-down model did not help and I hope that in the future staff in schools will have more say as to when they are involved.

As the number of ESG schemes had increased in this LEA, the problems associated with 'top-down' imposed INSET needed to be considered carefully by INSET planners. Solutions needed to be sought so as not to overburden and/or alienate the teachers, thus losing some of the undoubted benefits of the work of the ESG teams.

The LEA consultants, by responding to requests from the schools for help or information, avoided the dangers of imposition, but because of this some schools could have missed out on the expertise they offered. Some responses suggested that not all headteachers had sufficient information about consultants. One headteacher had the following suggestions: 'Headteachers to meet all authority consultants to hear briefly what they feel they can offer the schools and what time and resources they have available.' This is a reminder that effective and on-going communication should be an important priority of the LEA if opportunities are not to be missed or good work wasted.

Advisers were seen to have a unique role to play, having the chance to gain an overall view of national and LEA policies, a wide knowledge of many schools within the authority and a closer relationship with a few. 'A key involvement is the territorial adviser having a good relationship with the head in particular so that frank discussion might be held.' 'The advisers have to be objective observers, monitoring INSET in the context of the total school strategy and advising headteachers accordingly.'

Several headteachers wanted to be able to call upon relevant experts, whatever their official role – other teachers, staff from higher education, advisers, consultants – when their school perceived a need. One head put it as having 'available expertise to consult when needs are seen but the path is unclear'.

Only four headteachers referred to governors and parents and two stressed the need to interest them in and inform them of what was going on in the school. None saw at this stage a definite role for either group in the identification of needs. However, under the terms of the 1988 Education Reform Act, pressure from these two groups will increase in the future, adding to the considerable pressures already being felt in primary schools. It is necessary to consider whether these pressures for change and improvement are succeeding in achieving their aims or whether this headteacher's view is justified: 'Too many pressures from too many groups. These cannot possibly be responded to at the same time, in a beneficial and long-lasting way. More depth, consideration, resources and time are needed in each area to do them justice.'

Problems and difficulties encountered

Table 4.5 summarizes responses to the question that asked headteachers to indicate the difficulties they had encountered in the identification of needs in their school in the first year of the new LEA INSET funding arrangements.

As can be seen, 42 headteachers (63 per cent) felt that the process had highlighted so many areas of development that their staff were in danger of being overwhelmed. This is clearly a danger that must be guarded against and at other points in the questionnaire headteachers indicated their awareness of the need for early prioritization in the identification process. Thirty-six heads (54 per cent) felt that the process had raised expectations for professional developments that may be difficult

	Percentage of schools ($n = 67$)
1. Highlighted so many areas that staff are in danger of being overwhelmed	63
2. Raised expectations for professional development that may be difficult to meet	54
3. So time-consuming that it threatened to affect essential school activities	33
4. The confidence of some staff has been undermined	24
5. Some staff have been reluctant to participate	24
6. Failed to deal adequately with the professional development needs of individual teachers	22
7. It has contributed to lowering staff morale	12
8. It has become identical in some teachers' minds with appraisal	12

Table 4.5 Problems and difficulties encountered in needs identification

to meet. Linked with this are the fifteen cases (22 per cent) where headteachers felt that the process had, so far, failed to deal adequately with the professional development needs of individual teachers. These figures suggest that at that early stage of identifying and satisfying needs the focus was on the needs of the school rather than on the needs of the individual teacher. While this may be eminently desirable in many ways, if individual teachers have expectations aroused for professional development and those expectations are not met, the resulting disappointment and frustration may be a negative factor in whole-school development.

Only sixteen headteachers (24 per cent) felt that the

confidence of staff had been undermined and only eight (12 per cent) felt it had contributed to lowering staff morale. Although these figures are low they are still disturbing. They indicate that some teachers saw identifying needs as a means of finding fault with their professional performance, a way of criticizing present practice. The changes that are sought must be seen to be relevant to the improved education of the children, and the individual teacher must feel that he or she is fully involved as an equal partner in attempts to improve the learning of the pupils. In this regard, it is important to note that only five headteachers felt that the process had become identical in some teachers' minds with appraisal. Sixteen headteachers (24 per cent) indicated reluctance on the part of some staff to participate and in 22 schools (33 per cent) headteachers felt that the process had been so time-consuming that it threatened to affect the essential activities of the school.

Forty-one headteachers (61 per cent) added further comments on the question of difficulties and problems. Five wished to make it clear that they had not encountered any problems and so commented accordingly, two emphasizing the success of the process in their schools.

I have the contrary view based upon my staff's enthusiasm for INSET. None of the difficulties apply here. Teachers are willing to receive additional training and what is significant here in my school is that what they have learned is then given out to our other teachers in general discussions.

Eight headteachers (12 per cent) expressed more general disquiet about the effect of GRIST: it could become 'another disruption of children's education'. There could be 'so much traffic of teachers/advisers/co-ordinators/consultants coming into and out of school that it could have an unsettling effect on children'. Another headteacher worried 'that teachers leaving classes as part of their co-ordinating role or for other INSET activities are not fulfilling their prime function of being with the children whom they, of course, know better than anyone else'.

All this activity is regarded by 'some teachers as a cosmetic exercise' because 'previous experiences of INSET have not demonstrated to staff the positive effects one might expect training to have'. The INSET offered must be effective, not 'irrelevant, a waste of time', as a full-day course was considered to be by staff in one school. If real benefit cannot be seen after training, further identification of needs can only worsen the general situation and some of the most competent teachers will be further disheartened, as outlined by one head:

> The continual insistence upon in-service training is felt to imply criticism of the status quo, and, whilst the staff are not complacent, they are a very competent and hard-working group, producing excellent results; thus their morale is lowered by the implied criticism.

Eighteen headteachers (27 per cent) referred to lack of time and the proliferation of initiatives. As reported above, the identification of needs was seen by some heads to be time-consuming in itself and, since time is inevitably involved in responding to the identified need, their complaints were not surprising. 'Too much all at once', 'the initiatives have followed thick and fast', 'we are bombarded with ESG and other training schemes', 'stop the world, I want to get off!', give a flavour of the feelings expressed. But these are not just the understandable reactions of busy people being given even more to do. Their concern goes deeper than that. Because 'we are trying to do too much in too short a time', the benefits of the excellent work that was going on might be lost. The following comments illustrated their real anxiety:

> We really need a time for reflection and development or else the aim of all this, i.e. improving each child's education, will be lost.

> There is not time to see anything through thoroughly and completely.

> More time is needed to consolidate changes before embarking on new areas.

> The overloading of new initiatives has prevented any one being completed in depth.

It is difficult to set priorities, then devote the necessary time and thought to deal thoroughly with them.

The time-scale between one ESG support and other areas of consideration has been too little for proper evaluation and assessment for future development needs under GRIST/INSET.

The message seems clear: trying to do too much too quickly may in the end be worse than doing nothing. Establishing priorities and allowing sufficient time for them to be dealt with were essential if the hoped-for benefits were to materialize and real and lasting changes were to be made.

Gains made as a result of identifying INSET needs

Table 4.6 summarizes the information obtained from the question asking headteachers whether certain gains had been

	Percentage of schools ($n = 67$)
1. Increased staff awareness of different teaching methods	79
2. Improved staff awareness of the school's curriculum	73
3. A school-focused programme of INSET needs	61
4. Improved staff relationships	52
5. Accurately identified whole school INSET needs	45
6. Accurately identified areas of professional developments for individual staff	39
7. Thoroughly identified areas of weakness or deficit	31
8. Improved pupil–teacher relationships	16

Table 4.6 Benefits gained from the process of needs identification

made during the process of identifying needs. This question seemed to be more difficult to answer than any of the others in the questionnaire and for this reason the responses should be treated with caution.

Fifty-three headteachers (79 per cent) recorded that staff had an increased awareness of different teaching methods and 49 (73 per cent) recorded improved staff awareness of the school's curriculum. These are pleasing results to accrue from the identification of needs.

Only 41 headteachers (61 per cent) indicated that a school-focused programme of INSET activities had resulted from their identification of needs. It may be that this had still to be arranged or that difficulties were being encountered in arranging INSET appropriate to the identified needs of the school.

Only 30 heads (45 per cent) indicated that they had accurately identified whole school needs and only 21 (31 per cent) reported that they had thoroughly identified areas of weakness or deficit. This may indicate that headteachers had not been looking for areas of weakness or deficit as such, but had been approaching the exercise more positively in looking for ways to improve existing practice. It could also imply that some headteachers feel that areas of weakness or deficit exist to be more thoroughly identified.

A surprisingly small number (26 headteachers, 39 per cent) felt they had accurately identified areas of professional development for individual staff and this tied in with other data suggesting that the needs of individual teachers were not being met in all cases. Responses to an earlier question indicated that of the fairly small number of headteachers who used INSET questionnaires for each teacher and/or interviewed individual teachers formally about their INSET needs, over half found the approach most helpful. These may be efficient methods of identifying areas of professional development for individual staff, but identifying needs does not, of course, ensure that the identified needs are met.

Relationships are intangible and difficult to measure, and it is difficult to isolate any of the myriad factors that influence them.

However, the process of identifying needs can put relationships between staff under stress. It is therefore pleasing to note that 35 headteachers (52 per cent) felt able to record that identifying needs had improved staff relationships. Relationships with pupils can also be affected, to a degree depending perhaps on the methods used in the identification process, but only eleven headteachers (16 per cent) recorded an improvement; several were anxious to point out that staff–pupil relationships were already good.

Far fewer headteachers added to the list of suggested gains than added to the list of suggested difficulties and problems. This may be because headteachers feel that it was too early, in 1987, for benefits to be realized. 'Real curriculum development in a primary situation is a long process of assimilation and evaluation. Insufficient time has elapsed since the initiative began to make real value judgements on its effects, other than as a facile and simplistic response.' Although this view carries considerable weight, it is evident that government and LEA policies are demanding an approach that requires more speedy implementation of specific changes than that implied above. The first step in the INSET cycle is the identification of needs and it should be possible, if the process has been completed, to assess the outcomes, however limited or tentative they may be, of that process.

Six headteachers (9 per cent) *did* feel able to specify gains they felt had been made as a result of the identification of INSET needs. Four referred to the effects on staff:

It has helped to maintain morale by giving additional goals to teachers at a time when teachers feel very much undervalued.

Staff are becoming less resistant to change.

Greater professionalism visible amongst the staff.

Involvement of staff in curriculum appraisal and development.

One referred to the effect on pupils: 'Improved provision for the pupils in those areas which have been identified by the staff themselves.' Another felt it had 'improved relationships with neighbouring schools', while the final gain should be an important part of identifying needs – prioritization and the setting of reasonable goals: 'It has identified the limitations in achieving our aims under the constraints of present resources.' If limits are realized early enough, the pressure of trying to cope with too many objectives, and the disappointment when those objectives cannot be met, can both be reduced.

Help required with long term planning under GRIST
Table 4.7 contains the summarized results obtained from a question that asked headteachers to indicate whether any of the possibilities in a list would be especially useful to them in the longer term planning for INSET that is required under GRIST.

Forty-one headteachers (61 per cent) felt that grouping with other primary schools for planning purposes would be especially

	Percentage of schools (*n* = 67)
1. Grouping with other primary schools	61
2. A training course on long-term INSET needs identification and planning	58
3. Having access to an LEA specialist in every curriculum area	46
4. Closer liaison with LEA consultants	39
5. The appointment of a teacher with special responsibility for professional development	37
6. More regular meetings with LEA advisers and officers	33
7. Closer liaison with school advisers	33
8. Completing LEA questionnaires on long-term INSET needs	13

Table 4.7 Strategies to help headteachers in the long-term identification of needs

helpful. This reinforces the evidence that the links with other primary schools, already well-established in some cases, were found to be very helpful, but comments added suggest that some schools wished to be linked with schools of similar type or with similar needs – infants with infants, small school with small school, and so on.

Thirty-nine headteachers (58 per cent) recorded that a training course on long term INSET needs identification and planning would be especially useful to them 'if carefully structured and sensibly led'. Thirty-one (46 per cent) felt that having access to an LEA specialist in every major curriculum area would be helpful, with the provisos that 'they know sufficient to have a value' and that they 'have recent, relevant primary experience'.

Twenty-six headteachers (39 per cent) would have liked a closer liaison with LEA consultants, 22 (33 per cent) would like closer liaison with their school adviser(s) and 22 (33 per cent) would have liked more regular meetings with the LEA advisers and officers. This evidence suggests that for a fairly substantial number of these headteachers more support from the centre was desired.

Interestingly, 25 headteachers (37 per cent) would have found helpful the appointment in their school of a teacher with a special responsibility for professional development. This evidence suggests that a different structure from the whole-staff responsibility model, which has so far been adopted by 48 per cent of these headteachers (as shown in Figure 4.3), could develop in the future. However, primary teachers already carry many responsibilities and the existing allocation of allowances does not leave much room for additional responsibilities to be rewarded:

On top of other responsibilities and after a third of £501 allowances have been given to supply staff!

This is an onerous responsibility – the difficulty would be to give it the required status in the face of other demands.

In a small school where staff already have responsibility for two or more areas this would entail additional 'supply' time. I don't think I can ask anyone to take any more responsibility – all are class teachers with no 'non-contact' time.

One headteacher asserted that professional development was the headteacher's responsibility in primary schools; he or she of course has ultimate responsibility but demands on heads were already great and in 1987 seemed set to increase. In the face of the changes consequent upon the passing of the Education Reform Act, some re-allocation of responsibilities has been inevitable.

In all, 29 headteachers (43 per cent) made further suggestions and comments on ways of helping long term planning and eleven of these made direct reference to time and the necessity for more of it. They were rarely the same respondents who had commented that time was a problem in answer to an earlier question, so this emphasizes how widespread this concern was and continues to be. Some made positive suggestions for obtaining more time:

Less teaching commitment for primary headteachers to give more time to think about long term INSET needs (and to fill in INSET questionnaires).

Giving schools a chance to plan! The main resource which is always at a premium is time. Possibly the five days could profitably be used for this.

I honestly believe that one extra member of staff would be of more use than any other single step (e.g. take the headteacher out of all calculations for staffing establishment purposes).

Others expressed a more general concern about the failure to consolidate if more time was not found or initiatives spread out: 'To be left alone to consolidate dynamic curriculum initiatives in maths, science/technology and computers in education.' Two headteachers were blunter:

If you want a good job doing then time, courses, extra staff and money are needed. Unless and until these are adequately provided and the plethora of demands reduced, you will end up with cosmetic changes only.

Headteachers are normally aware of the INSET needs of their school but time is the main factor. One is also aware of a class teacher being away from their class too often. One also wonders if this has ever occurred to consultants, advisers, co-ordinators, etc., as they justify their own existence with spurious forms, surveys and questionnaires.

Some headteachers expressed a desire for more information about the long term plans of the LEA: 'Information on the curriculum areas and initiatives which the LEA will be considering over the next 3 years – especially whether time and resources will be allocated (e.g. ESG schemes) or whether schools have to provide this.' 'A three-year course plan based on LEA questionnaire.' Another headteacher wanted more clarity and prescription from the LEA: 'A more clearly defined policy for INSET on the part of the LEA would be eminently useful. There are too many generalization policies from the LEA. Policies should be much more prescriptive and therefore helpful to already over-burdened primary heads!'

Examples of actual needs identified

The headteachers were asked to outline briefly the steps taken by their schools to identify needs in one particular area of the curriculum. One aspect of the GRIST approach to primary schools was that it tended to be subject-based as in the secondary school model, whereas practice and philosophy in many primary schools made this seem inappropriate, but only one headteacher pointed out that that school did not look at needs in terms of a subject-based curriculum.

Twenty-two headteachers (33 per cent) chose mathematics and twelve (18 per cent) chose science. Other subjects chosen were religious education, language, computers, humanities, special needs, reading, sex education, art, physical education and information technology. The preponderance of examples from mathematics and science may be a result of the ESG schemes, although few mentioned ESG participation. It may instead reflect their interest in these fields; only six heads gave language as their example.

The major needs identified ranged from the very specific ('place value') to the more general ('we felt we were doing insufficient work on logic and problem solving'). One example illustrates some of the processes and effects involved:

(a) *Curriculum area*
Mathematics

(b) *Steps taken to identify needs*
(i) ESG scheme
(ii) Individuals looking at themselves
(iii) Meetings where problems are brought out
(iv) Collective help and support

(c) *Major need identified*
Being too close and having too little time.

(d) *How that need is being met*
We are beginning to talk about problems and finding that perhaps an area we have taken for granted may have an alternative approach.

The meeting of the needs identified seemed in most cases well advanced and ranged from staff attending courses to the purchase of new books and equipment, although some headteachers felt it was too early to be definite about meeting the needs identified.

Conclusions to the study

From the evidence gathered from the completed questionnaires we concluded that the successful identification of INSET needs in primary schools is dependent on the following:

- The active participation of the whole staff in examining whole-school needs.
- The adequate identification of the professional development needs of the individual teacher through formal or informal interview, through school-devised INSET questionnaires or through other means specifically designed for this purpose.
- Some formal structure of responsibility to facilitate co-ordination and prioritization. If INSET is given a high priority by the LEA, those who take responsibility for it must have the time to exercise that responsibility adequately. In many primary schools as presently organized no teacher, not even the headteacher, has enough time to take on this role.

- A clear LEA policy on the balance between the external identification of needs and school-based identification of needs. Schools need to know whether, if they feel that attempts to meet externally identified needs are inappropriate or mistimed, negotiation can take place to adapt or re-time the external initiative.
- Information about LEA policy and provision of INSET as far in advance as possible, in as much detail as possible, and information about how that will affect individual schools.
- Information about sources of INSET in a brief, manageable form with addresses, telephone numbers, etc., and about how different sources are funded.
- Earlier and more frequent contact with those involved in INSET, i.e. advisers and consultants. Face-to-face contact seems much more effective than paper communication.

Review

The identification of INSET needs is neither a cosmetic activity nor something that can be undertaken in a mechanical way. If it is done badly then the provision of INSET and the evaluation of its effects will also be less efficient and worthwhile. There are difficulties in defining precisely what a training need is and in determining priorities over time and within agendas that are increasingly being set at some distance from the teacher in his or her classroom. National priorities and local priorities often seem to overshadow the needs of individual schools and groups and individuals within schools. However, while it is easy to assert the importance of developing effective methods of identifying needs, it is clear that any effective method requires two things that schools currently lack: the availability of time for INSET co-ordinators and others to fulfil their roles in this regard, and the appropriate administrative support to keep adequate records and to monitor the steps from seeking to identify needs to translation of the needs into provision. These difficulties are well-illustrated in the information gathered from the primary school study reported in this chapter. What follows in the next chapters, which focus on INSET provision, assumes that adequate methods of identifying needs have been used.

5 Courses

For many teachers, INSET planners and providers, the word 'course' is the first thing to come to mind when INSET is being discussed. As we shall read in the next chapter, there are many alternatives to courses. However, in this chapter the focus will be initially on the distinctive features of INSET courses; later, detailed consideration is given to the way in which traditional course providers are adjusting to the new INSET funding arrangements.

Before the introduction of TRIST, GRIST and LEATGS, an important distinction was made between a 'long' course and a 'short' course. The distinction was important for teachers, LEAs and providers since it determined whether or not the costs of course attendance could be paid from money in the DES pool. Pooling enabled an LEA to pass on all or part of the cost of an INSET activity to the LEAs collectively. The argument was that spending from the pool should have brought benefits to the education service generally. For course attendance to be subsidized or paid from the pool, which was held by the DES, a course had to involve attendance of at least 20 days full-time or 60 hours part-time. Such long courses were to be provided in institutions of further or higher education and approved lists of such courses were published annually in the DES *Handbook of Long Courses*. Exceptions to this were courses offered in a distance learning mode and teacher fellowships, which were also funded from the pool.

Short courses were not funded from the pool. They were defined as any courses which were less than 20 days full-time or 60 hours part-time. The ending of the pooling arrangements saw the end of the long–short distinction and the modification by the providers of their course provision.

The key features of a course that distinguish it from such activities as workshops and conferences are that it is made up of more than one meeting and that it is usually attended by more than one teacher. As with any other form of curriculum activity, an INSET course can be defined by its aims and objectives, content, teaching and learning methods, and mode of assessment. An ideal course would be planned so carefully that there would be no ambiguity in the way these aspects were described. Achieving the match between the providers' definitions of aims, content, teaching and learning methods and modes of assessment and those of the teachers intending to attend a course is not straightforward. It is the mismatch between the individual course attender's perceptions of the intentions of the provider and the expectations and assumptions of the client in the mind of the provider that lies at the heart of much dissatisfaction with the course as the most appropriate vehicle for providing INSET.

There is no shortage of advice on how to avoid the most obvious pitfalls. Rudduck (1981) pinpoints a number of key issues:

Who should plan the course?
The course advertisement.
The aims of the course.
Orientation.
Timing.
Structure and style.
Participation.
Continuity.
Setting.
Resources.

Similarly, Robson *et al.* (1988), as a result of their research into the effectiveness of INSET courses in the field of special education, offer a checklist for short course providers:

1. The starting point is a need. A course may not be the best way of meeting the need.

115

2. It is important that the need is seen and expressed by the teachers forming the target audience.
3. A one-off course is unlikely to be effective. Follow-up activities are important. A course should be part of a wider programme of planned development.
4. The teachers for whom the course is intended should play a part in determining its objectives and content.
5. Effective courses are ones which lead to changes in practice. Follow-up support is necessary for this to take place. Active involvement of the headteacher is crucial.
6. Resources from the local authority to support involvement with courses and activities arising from them are needed, not only for the direct effect but also to legitimate these activities.
7. Courses involving teachers from different schools (or authorities) need to recognize the different settings to which they return. If more than one teacher from a particular school (or authority) attends they can provide mutual support.
8. Effectiveness is increased if, during the course and afterwards, teachers can and actually do interact with each other, share ideas and help one another.
9. The course leader is responsible for ensuring that each stage of the planning and implementation of a short course has been carefully thought through.
10. Without some form of evaluation you have no way of assessing the effectiveness of a course.

The work of Rudduck and that of Robson and his colleagues indicates that a short course requires very careful preparation on the part of both the teachers and the providers. To acknowledge that courses stem from the identified needs of individual teachers is to make an assertion about the importance of negotiation between the providers and the teachers, and there is evidence that this negotiation is now commonplace. This is not to suggest, however, that speculative courses are on the way out. For the provider there remains the difficulty associated with the short timescale between deciding to provide a particular INSET activity and gaining the support of LEAs and teachers for it. The more that providers offer speculative courses the more they are accused of employing an out-dated top-down model. The alternative to this model, in which all the parameters of the course are determined by the provider, is a model based on thorough negotiation in which the provider must wait for an invitation from an LEA, a school or a group of teachers to begin negotiations. The use of a tendering system using the kind of pro-forma illustrated in Figure 5.1 facilitates this introductory stage.

This pro-forma is useful for a school INSET co-ordinator who, having identified a training need, wishes to arrange an appropriate form of INSET for a group of teachers and is unclear about the best way of providing it. The form is sent to a number of providers and the information so obtained serves as the starting point for more formal negotiation. Once an idea that may be in the minds of teachers, planners or providers has been articulated, there are three major stages in course design: pre-course; in-course; and post-course. Each stage requires close attention by the providers and the teachers.

Pre-course, there are two principal stages. The first step is to define training needs as sharply as possible. Then there is a negotiation procedure, in which intermediaries, such as LEA advisers and school INSET co-ordinators, may be closely involved in discussions with potential providers. It is at this preliminary stage that the assumptions, expectations and intentions of the teachers and the providers are brought to the surface and discussed in detail. In the negotiations matters of principle and practice will be considered. With regard to principles, there will be a discussion of course aims and how these can be prioritized. The definition of aims will lead to a consideration of content and training methods. Underpinning any negotiations will be considerations of time and costs. When these have been taken into account the operational details of a course can be worked out. These details will include number of participants, venue, resource materials, staffing, duration, timing and accreditation.

Following the preliminary negotiation stage comes the planning stage, when the structure of a course is constructed, preferably as a continuation of the earlier negotiations. The

INSET Activity Request

1. Subject: ....
2. Target (For which teachers/teaching which students. No. of teachers.):   ....
3. Level (Novices/training of teachers): ....
4. Format (full-time/part-time/school-based): ....
5. Aims: ....
6. Award/credit required: ....
7. Timing (term, month, day(s), time(s), rolling programme, one-off):   ....
8. Starting date: ....
9. Venue (school, teachers' centre, university): ....
10. Estimated cost (principal cost items): .... £ .... £ .... £ ....
11. If you are unable to provide, please could you recommend another   provider: ....
12. Proposer: Name .... Phone ....   School address ....

Date: ....

Figure 5.1   An example of a pro-forma used to initiate course
negotiation.

118

structure will indicate the course syllabus, including how the course will be presented. It should pay close attention to the teaching methods to be employed during the course and spell out what will be expected of the teachers in addition to simply attending the course.

Once the course structure has been planned the next step is to nominate or recruit the course participants. When the course membership is clear attention must be paid to any preparation the teachers must make before attending the first course meeting. Such preparation may take the form of reading, watching videos, listening to audio cassettes, writing accounts of classroom experiences or collecting relevant documentation, such as textbooks, pupil worksheets, examples of pupils' work, syllabuses and tests.

When the pre-course stage is complete the course will commence. There are three sub-stages in the presentation of the course. There is an initiating or orientation stage, when the operation of the course will be explained to course attenders and further negotiation may take place regarding the details of the course. At this stage expectations and assumptions will be further clarified and rapport will be established among the course attenders and between them and the providers. With the ground rules for the course established the course can evolve over its allotted time. The methods employed will vary according to the course aims. Providers have access to a wide range of training methods and, depending on the length of a course, it is likely that a variety of methods will be employed. A key issue is the kind of participation expected of the course attenders. Group discussions, syndicates working on tasks, simulations and training games, school visits, classroom observation, and the use of audio-visual aids are part of the trainers' repertoire. There is commonly a tension in deciding how much time in a course should be given over to the sharing of experience between the course attenders and how much given to the transmission by the course presenter of new information or skills. It is not unusual to hear teachers complain about the excessive use of active learning methods in some INSET courses.

119

Some providers are surprised to hear teachers asking for more formal presentation of information. Clearly, much depends on the nature of the course, i.e. the kind of content and the expectations of teachers and planners.

Once the stage of course attendance has been completed there comes the follow-up stage. This may take the form of support for individual teachers in their own work places. It may also take the form of one or more refresher courses attended by the same group that took the course. In some cases attendance at another course, closely associated with the initial one, may be appropriate.

The accreditation of INSET

In order to understand the responses made by higher education (HE) institutions to the new arrangements for INSET, we can identify some of their traditional accreditation practices and then reflect on the contributions that HE might make to an emerging INSET framework. It is important to focus on accreditation since this is one of the distinguishing features of INSET provision in universities, polytechnics and colleges of higher education. It would be helpful if HE institutions were homogeneous in their INSET structures and processes but it is obvious that this is not the case. It is possible to generalize about some of the responses made to the changing structures and processes of INSET and to place these responses in the context of accreditation. Institutions of HE may accredit their own courses, as is the case generally in universities, courses may be accredited by an outside body, as is the case for many polytechnics and colleges of higher education, which have their courses accredited by the CNAA (Council for National Academic Awards), or they may accredit courses organized and taught elsewhere. Associated with the word accreditation are the notions of credit recognition, credit accumulation, credit exemption and credit transfer. I shall comment on how these credit arrangements are being introduced. In doing so I shall begin with the experience of some university departments of education (UDEs), then move to a consortium context that embraces trans-binary initiatives and finally consider the national perspective.

Individual UDEs

Traditionally, UDEs have distinguished sharply between award-bearing and non-award-bearing INSET activities. Indeed, the term INSET was often used solely in the context of the latter and award-bearing courses were perceived as something different. To some extent this reflected the distinction made between the work of the ATOs (Area Training Organizations), which were responsible for the validation of courses provided in the former colleges of education, and local INSET provision, which was seen as a contribution made by the universities to their local and regional communities. The provision of the universities' own award-bearing courses was made by the UDEs. One of the results of the current LEATGS arrangements has been the conflation of award-bearing and non-award-bearing INSET activities in UDEs and a re-definition of the concept of INSET in universities as a whole.

Within UDEs, there was a tradition of providing part-time and full-time courses at a number of levels. While most UDEs provide a PGCE course of initial teacher training, they have also provided an array of taught certificate, diploma and master's courses, in addition to research awards. It would be wrong to suggest that before LEATGS, UDEs had established a neat, coherent ladder of awards. The words 'certificate' and 'diploma', in particular, are used differently within individual UDEs and between UDEs. This diversity of definition provides the basis for a fluid pattern of course provision within a UDE but poses serious difficulties when any inter-institutional collaboration is contemplated. For the potential student and for the agencies responsible for paying fees, the complexity of current provision is far from helpful.

The levels referred to above had evolved as a way of easing matriculation to further advanced courses. Entry to a taught master's course was, and still is in some UDEs, dependent on acquiring success or a specified level of success in a previous course, e.g. a diploma in the advanced study of education. The in-service route for advanced study, of diploma end-on to taught master's degree, has been a popular part-time sequence of studies for ambitious British teachers. The full-time master's consequent upon a part-time diploma was popularized through the DES pooling arrangements, which enabled local education authorities to second quite large numbers of teachers to UDEs. These LEA-sponsored teacher numbers were supplemented by full-time overseas students. The pooling arrangements also facilitated the introduction of non-award-bearing courses in such fields as science education, mathematics education, special education and school management, following DES Circular 3/83. The courses that were undertaken in some UDEs have proved to be an important ingredient in some of the new course structures that have emerged since the introduction of GRIST.

Within the diploma and master's part-time courses the convention was for teachers to attend classes in a UDE for two hours per week for two terms for two years, followed, at master's level, by a further year when a dissertation would be written. This led to the four-unit design of master's programmes. Unconventional arrangements were courses offered at a distance by the Open University and courses that concentrated teaching into a number of weekends rather than a series of evenings.

GRIST and LEATGS have seen a number of significant changes in this traditional pattern in, probably, most UDEs. The scale of the change varies from one UDE to another. In some the changes mark a distinct departure from what had existed before, in others the changes simply accelerated a process that was already under way.

The most obvious changes can be detected in the responses made to the sharp reduction in full-time, one-year secondments by LEAs. UDEs recognized the need to design courses that could be studied by teachers who, instead of studying full-time for one year, wished to study on the basis of half-day, one-day or one-term release. The neat divide between part-time and full-time modes of study was no longer appropriate. Furthermore, there was a need to extend the length of courses, permitting teachers to complete their studies in a time span longer than the conventional three years for part-time courses. The possibility of new attendance patterns called for a reconsideration of the conventional two-term taught course unit and this has led to the introduction of modular course structures. It is only a short step from the design of a modular structure to the identification within that structure of unified, coherent, sequenced courses of study, or 'pick and mix' arrangements and of self-standing course units appropriate for teachers not wishing to follow a full, award-bearing course. The disaggregation of courses has raised the issue of awarding credit for the completion of a number of course units, or modules, which are fewer in number than those needed for the award for which the units were initially designed.

As we have seen, the principal thrust of LEATGS has been the provision of INSET activities, not necessarily courses, that match the identified needs of individual teachers, functional groups, consortia of schools, whole schools and LEAs. The notion that academics can simply design whatever courses they see fit and advertise these in a speculative way to potential students has been challenged, to be replaced by the notion of negotiation. Such negotiation seeks to bring out the close matching of identified INSET needs and INSET provision.

Just as changes have been introduced in the timing of course delivery and the re-organization of INSET course structures, so have changes been made in the content of courses and in their modes of assessment. In addition, changes are occurring in the place where INSET is being delivered. The pressure on INSET providers to make available relevant, differentiated, coherent, school-based and school-focused INSET activities has increased with the introduction of LEATGS, and this has led to some interesting experiments.

An example which illustrates many of these changes can be taken from a course developed in one university. The course structure is shown in Figure 5.2. Route 4 in the diagram can be

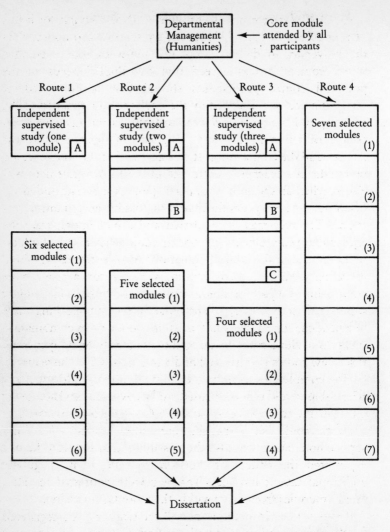

Figure 5.2   Modular Course Arrangements for an M Ed degree.

viewed as a conventional route for a student following a course leading to the award of the M Ed (Educational Studies) degree. It comprises eight taught modules (derived from a pre-existing, conventional four-unit taught M Ed) followed by a dissertation.

124

An LEA adviser sought to provide an INSET course for heads of humanities in the LEA's secondary schools and approached the university to discuss a possible ten-week, one evening a week, course. It was agreed that the INSET needs of the potential course participants should first be identified. A questionnaire was designed by the adviser and circulated to the schools, and the responses were collated. From this evidence a course of ten meetings was designed collaboratively by the adviser and the course tutor. It was agreed that the course would be taught in a teachers' centre within the LEA. Agreement was also reached on the number of participants, the timing and mode of delivery. At this point the matter of possible accreditation was raised. Ten meetings, each of two and a half hours, were the equivalent requirements to one module within the modular M Ed course in the UDE. Regulations for the degree permitted a teacher to devise, in consultation with a tutor, a programme comprising taught modules and up to three independent supervised study modules. The possibility of undertaking these independent supervised study modules, alone or in combination (i.e. two or three could be merged to constitute one), opened up three new routes (Routes 1, 2 and 3 in Figure 5.2). The teachers, having completed successfully the core module, could engage in school-based and school-focused studies, with supervision being given in the teachers' own schools. Clusters, or syndicates, of teachers could be established for joint studies and joint supervision. There was also the possibility that the LEA, having negotiated the details of the core module, could negotiate additional taught modules. Teachers were permitted to select taught modules from those within the modular provision.

It was acknowledged that not all the teachers who registered for the core module would wish to continue their studies beyond that module. It was also acknowledged that some of the teachers might be interested in intermediary awards, e.g. certificates or diplomas, on the successful completion of specified numbers of modules, although this was not possible at that time. Regulations did, however, permit students to follow a part-time M Ed course over a period of six years. This has implications for the teachers who, in that period, might change their jobs not only in geographical terms but also in terms of their position on the career ladder. The choice of modules could be delayed and this would accommodate the career change. To allow for a change in job location it was necessary to plan for credit transfer.

This example has served to highlight the importance of negotiated course structures. The structure described incorporates modularization, taught and independent supervised study modules, extended courses, LEA-located and school-based studies, credit accumulation and the need for credit transfer. Other examples can be found in other UDEs. Reading the course publicity materials from such universities as Liverpool, Newcastle, Sheffield and Southampton indicates how far some UDEs have progressed towards the establishment of course arrangements that incorporate credit recognition and credit accumulation.

The diversity and variety of traditional UDE course provision have been retained in contemporary course revision. Each UDE is progressing in its own way, providing distinct patterns that reflect local circumstances. From the UDEs mentioned in the previous paragraph we can highlight a number of patterns. Liverpool has introduced a Certificate in the Advanced Study of Education, which is achieved through credit accumulation, with some course units being taught in LEAs by LEA staff. The award of this certificate can earn exemption from up to two modules of a higher award. At Newcastle there is a Modular Diploma in Advanced Educational Studies, which is constructed on the basis of a combination of short courses, long courses, options and core courses. Sheffield has introduced a credit aggregation scheme, which envelops certificate, diploma and master's awards and which can include special programmes for LEAs, schools and individuals. Southampton has a credit transfer system for a Diploma in Advanced Educational Studies, comprising four Certificates of Advanced Educational Studies, which permits transfer between the university, affiliated public sector institutions and the Open University.

Consortia

It is clear that developments currently taking place in INSET provision in UDEs could not be understood without a careful analysis of LEATGS and the interactions between UDEs, LEAs, schools and teachers. Equally, account must be taken of developments taking place in individual universities, the university sector of higher education, and higher education as a whole.

Central government policies for higher education have been most clearly expressed in the Green Paper, *The Development of Higher Education into the 1990s* (1985), and the White Paper, *Higher Education: Meeting the Challenge*, which was published in April 1987. The policy proposals contained in these documents were designed to: make more effective use of the resources available for higher education; maintain and where possible enhance standards; continue to expand and broaden access; encourage higher education to be better managed, more flexible and more attuned to the needs of industry and commerce. In 1982, the Department of Education and Science had launched the PICKUP (Professional, Industrial and Commercial Updating) Programme. The aim of PICKUP was to help colleges, polytechnics and universities to increase and improve the work they did in meeting the adult updating and retraining needs of employers and their employees. The type of training envisaged in PICKUP was: specifically vocational; for those in employment; post-experience; collaborative between higher education and employers; short, part-time, flexible and cost-effective; and self-financing. With regard to preferred mode of delivery, the emphasis was upon: short-course and bespoke training packages; action learning; independent study, including programmes of open or distance learning; in-house or on-site training; and consultancy and research. One of the products of the introduction of PICKUP has been the establishment of regional consortia.

Coventry consortium was the first to be set up under the aegis of PICKUP. Comprising Warwick University, Coventry Polytechnic and three colleges of further education, it was established on a pilot basis in 1983. Since then several other PICKUP consortia have been established. The South East England Consortium for Credit Transfer (SEEC) encompasses a number of public sector institutions of higher education drawn from a region that extends from Brighton through London to Oxford. The aims of SEEC are of particular interest in the context of INSET accreditation. They have been listed as:

To extend access to higher education to all those able to benefit from it.

To develop a comprehensive Continuing Education system in the region.

To facilitate non-standard entry.

To provide a counselling service for students.

To extend the provision of diverse and flexible modes of study, including Associated Student Schemes, intercalated work experience, independent study and distance learning.

To improve student access and develop credit transfer by liaising with other institutions, including universities, validating bodies and colleges of further education.

An important feature of the proposed credit transfer arrangements in SEEC is the concept of the 'consortium credit'. This has been defined as a 120th part of a full-time year of study at degree level. Course units could be given a credit rating with a three-year full-time undergraduate degree course being calibrated at 360 consortium credits. SEEC went on to define a series of levels of study to which were accorded a number of credit units. This structure was adopted by the CNAA-initiated Credit Accumulation and Transfer Scheme (CATS). As we shall see later, this structure has been adopted for the purpose of developing a credit transfer agreement by the Universities Council for the Education of Teachers (UCET).

Developments in SEEC and CATS were carefully monitored in a Leverhulme funded study of in-course credit recognition, sponsored by the Consortium of Advanced Continuing Education and Training (CONTACT), which brings together the Universities of Manchester and Salford, UMIST, the Manchester Business School and Manchester Polytechnic

(Williams 1987). The aims of CONTACT are: to increase the quantity and to improve the quality of adult learning opportunities in the North-West; to improve access to part-time and continuing education and training; and to co-ordinate and make more resource-effective the provision of continuing education and training. These aims have been translated into six specific consortium objectives:

1. Achieving collaboration in the provision of continuing education and training, e.g. by credit transfer and joint programming.
2. Providing a central information and reference point.
3. Joint marketing of provision of continuing education and training and joint market research activities.
4. Representation of the common interests of the Four (now Five) at regional, national and international levels – to governmental and EEC agencies, to industrial, professional and commercial organizations, to other suppliers of continuing education and training.
5. Developing central expertise, e.g. in sources of funding for continuing education and training.
6. Providing a focus for development projects, e.g. on new forms of provision.

CONTACT has been active in promoting: the extension of part-time undergraduate and postgraduate degree programmes: the modularization, where appropriate, of existing and new courses, and credit transfer between the member institutions; more research-based training programmes; and an increase in the number of mature students entering full- or part-time post-experience vocational education courses.

In the context of INSET in CONTACT it is worth referring briefly to the modular Diploma in Special Education Needs (Regional Scheme), which is collaboratively taught at Manchester Polytechnic and the University of Manchester. This diploma has been validated in parallel by both the CNAA and the University of Manchester and there is also a joint validating mechanism for one part of the course. Students must choose to register at either the Polytechnic or the University. This trans-binary, inter-institutional collaboration is an interesting

129

example of in-course credit recognition, i.e. the inter-institutional recognition of courses such as to produce joint teaching for one qualification. The establishment of consortia provides a useful infrastructure for facilitating the introduction of in-course credit recognition although, as I have indicated elsewhere, there are thirteen principal issues that need to be addressed in designing courses that permit such recognition. These issues are: academic standards; calibration of course units; course coherence; student numbers; compatibility of entry requirements to course units; compatibility of regulations; examinations; student access to institutional facilities; fees; liaison between academic staff; publicity and information; counselling of staff and students; and harmonization of timetables.

Award	Level	Credit (no. of CONTACT credit units)
Doctorate	1	120
Master's	2	120
	1	120
Postgraduate Diploma	2	120
	1	120
Postgraduate Certificate	2	120
	1	120
Undergraduate Degree	6	120
	5	120
	4	120
	3	120
	2	120
	1	120
Diploma of Higher Education	2	120
	1	120
Access courses		

Table 5.1 A proposed inter-institutional credit transfer scheme

For CONTACT, I proposed an inter-institutional credit transfer scheme, based on in-course credit recognition, which would cover the principal awards available to students in the consortium. This scheme is shown in Table 5.1.

It is important to recognize that the 120 CONTACT credit units allocated to any one level must not be taken to be equivalent to 120 CONTACT credit units at any other level. The concept of level is crucial to an understanding of the credit worthiness of a course unit. Reference to 120 CONTACT credit units without a preceding attribution of those units to a specific level renders the units meaningless for the purpose of credit transfer. The selection of 120 as the appropriate number of units at each level was determined by the structure of units created by SEEC and CATS.

National initiatives

Reference has already been made to the CNAA CAT Scheme. The Scheme has four priorities:

> To operate a personal advisory service for students at the Council's London offices on the credit rating of qualifications and experience which they already possess.

> To support links between consortia established to promote credit accumulation and continuing professional development.

> To act as an 'academic broker' in relation to the education and training needs of industry.

> To promote continuing professional education.

The Scheme was formally launched in 1986 and it operates under the CNAA's published regulations for award-bearing courses at all levels. The relevance of CATS for INSET accreditation lies not only in the calibration structure that CATS devised but also in the attention paid to credit exemption arrangements, which took account of both qualifications and experience. This reference to experience raises a whole range of problems with regard to INSET. I have already referred to the development within UDEs of schemes, such as those in

131

Liverpool, Sheffield and Newcastle, that incorporate short-course credit recognition within a credit ladder of qualifications. The possibility of giving credit exemption on the basis of professional experience introduces a substantially different dimension to the discussion. We shall return to this aspect near the end of this chapter.

CATS is of particular relevance to UDEs in that the credit transfer arrangements at its foundation were used as a keystone for the UCET Credit Transfer Agreement for master's level courses. It is worth noting that UCET established a Working Party on Credits, which, as far back as 1976, reported that: 'INSET is becoming increasingly part-time and courses, therefore, last much longer than their full-time equivalents', and went on to recommend that:

> Universities contemplating introducing a credit system should use as a basic credit unit a module which would form one-sixth of a one-year full-time course, i.e. in a full-time course a module demanding all the student's effort for half a term would gain one credit. The student would, therefore, need six credits to qualify for the award. We would expect to see double-credit (and maybe treble-credit) courses, particularly where the system chosen consisted of a common core plus options. Similarly, there would be no objection to half-credit courses.

More than a decade later another Modules/Credits Working Party was set up by UCET and this reported in 1987. The immediate product of this working party was the UCET Credit Transfer Agreement for taught master's degree courses, which was circulated to UDEs in March 1988. The text of the agreement is reproduced in Figure 5.3. The working party had acknowledged that 'the opportunity to establish a unified system based upon a basic module had been lost or individual universities had evolved or were evolving their own distinctive course structures'.

The working party sought to recommend a system, or framework, that would be established on a number of key principles. First, it should encompass both pre-course credit recognition (transfer with advanced standing) and in-course credit recognition (credit borrowing). Secondly, the system should be non-prescriptive, giving students credit for course work completed but no automatic right of entry to another

UNIVERSITIES COUNCIL FOR THE EDUCATION OF TEACHERS (UCET)
UCET CREDIT TRANSFER SCHEME

A. RATIONALE

A.1. This information is intended to facilitate the establishment of a credit transfer scheme initially between universities and subsequently across the binary line, enabling a student to be awarded a taught master's degree in education by successful study in more than one institution.

A.2. The scheme is designed for credit transfer within taught master's courses. It encompasses transfer with advanced standing and in-course credit recognition. It is entirely a matter for each university in the scheme (a) to decide whether or not to register a student seeking transfer, and (b) to be responsible for the overall coherence of a student's course of study. The scheme is arranged to accommodate modular and non-modular courses. Credit transfer will normally be permitted only for taught components and will exclude dissertations.

B. THE SCHEME

B.1. A taught master's degree course is deemed to carry 120 UCET credit units (UCUs). UCUs are measures of the assessment of constituent parts of total courses.

B.2. The minimum amount of credit available for transfer is 10 UCUs.

B.3. The maximum amount of credit normally available for transfer is 40 UCUs, i.e. one third of the total course units.

B.4. A standard master's transcript will be used as a record of a student's accumulation of credit.

In order to introduce the scheme universities were invited to fulfil a number of tasks:

(a) ensure that there were appropriate regulations for permitting credit transfer in taught master's courses;

(b) establish the credit-worthiness of each of the constituent parts of the taught master's course;

(c) incorporate details of such credit-worthiness in course prospectuses;

(d) include explanation of advanced standing and in-course credit recognition procedures in course prospectuses;

(e) institute the use of the standard master's transcript as a record of a student's accumulation of credit;

(f) establish an internal mechanism for the consideration of credit transfer with advanced standing and in-course credit recognition for potential and registered students.

Figure 5.3   Universities Council for the Education of Teachers (UCET) Credit Transfer Scheme.

course in another institution. Here, the essential distinction was made between course recognition and student recognition. It was envisaged that universities would continue to decide which students would be permitted to register for their courses. Thirdly, in providing courses that were in the best interests of individual students course coherence ought to be taken into account and this embraced course content, teaching methods, modes of assessment and the ethos of the institution.

Six criteria for a credit transfer system at master's level were proposed and these have relevance for courses at other levels. First, it needed to be comprehensive and easily understood by academic staff and students. Secondly, it should be simple to administer, in the interests of time and cost. Thirdly, it should be comprehensive in coverage and sufficiently flexible to accommodate short courses, part-time and full-time modes of attendance, taught courses and courses that include taught components, projects and dissertations. Fourthly, it should be compatible with credit systems existing or developing elsewhere, e.g. CATS and the Open University. Fifthly, it should accommodate modular and non-modular course structures. Finally, it should not inhibit innovation in course development.

It was recommended that, at the discrete master's level, a level sharply distinguished from other levels of work, there should be ascribed 120 UCET credit units. A unit was defined as the measure of the assessment of a part of the total course. It was not a measure of attendance and should not be equated with an amount of time given over to teaching. It was left for each university to allocate credit units to each examinable component of its courses, including the dissertation. It was recommended that the 'rule of the two-thirds' should be adopted for advanced standing and credit borrowing purposes, i.e. transfer should be permitted, *ad hominem*, for no more than one-third of a course.

Behind the brevity of the UCET Credit Transfer Agreement lies a more detailed report, which had been the basis for a series of formal discussions within UCET. It became clear that the agreement would have implications for other levels of work within UDEs. In this regard it is important to notice the confusion that exists in the terminology used by UDEs to title courses. Thus the term 'diploma' covers courses of varying levels, lengths, aims, content, teaching methods and modes of assessment. Some are used as preparation for more advanced courses, while others are fall-back awards for students who, having registered for a master's degree course, subsequently wish to terminate their studies earlier than the normal completion time. The same is true of some certificates. Attempts by some universities to construct credit ladders in which students can accumulate credit by following a coherent sequence of course units, or aggregate credit by adding together disparate units that eventually lead to an award, have produced grey areas between the various awards that constitute the rungs in the ladder. This greyness is best illustrated by the credit exemption regulations that have been introduced by some UDEs.

Credit exemption has raised some interesting issues for those UDEs that have sought to give credit exemption for success in short INSET courses provided in other institutions. Such credit recognition is usually not straightforward, not least because it is usual for universities to recognize not only courses but also the teachers of those courses. Beyond the recognition of INSET not taught by university staff on university premises, there are problems associated with giving credit for professional experience which has not been linked to attendance at formal courses. Essential to both these issues is the need to decide precisely what it is that universities are engaged in when they recognize credit. Traditionally universities have jealously guarded what they have perceived to be the standards of work that distinguish their courses from those in other institutions. The terms 'undergraduate' and 'postgraduate' are not used lightly. Thus the term 'level', when applied in the context of credit attribution, is a crucial term. There are levels of work (sub-undergraduate) that are not normally undertaken in universities. From this we can see that universities can only accredit those activities that lead to measures of success defined by those criteria that are applied to their own intra-institutional activities. Moves towards a client-centred model of INSET, in

135

which employer-provided training and client-centred training have become central components, have challenged the conventional accreditation arrangements. In recent years UDEs have introduced flexible, innovatory structures for the delivery of INSET. There is evidence of UDEs exploring changes in their policies and practices with regard to access, timetabling, location, use of new technologies for course presentation, modularization and credit transfer and exemption. They are also experiencing difficulties in translating the theoretical under-pinnings of the client-centred INSET model into practice.

6 Alternatives to courses

The importance attributed to alternatives to courses in the professional development of teachers acknowledges that, traditionally, only a very small number of teachers attended short or long INSET courses in any year. Even with an expansion of opportunities for course attendance consequent upon the availability of TRIST, GRIST and LEATGS funding, there are many difficulties in the way of increasing teacher attendance. In some LEAs it is proving extremely difficult to provide adequate teacher cover for those teachers who wish to be absent from school to attend INSET courses. Many teachers are reluctant to leave their classes in order to attend courses. What has become obvious in the programmes arranged for the preparation of teachers for the National Curriculum is that teachers' expectations cannot be met in full through INSET course provision. In the light of these and other factors there is a need for more and more attention to be paid to alternatives to courses as the principal vehicles for providing professional development.

Too sharp a focus on courses, conferences and workshops underestimates the professional experience gained by teachers through a variety of other means. Clearly, teachers benefit from their day-to-day conversations and more formal exchanges and discussions with colleagues in school corridors, staff rooms and committee rooms. They also gather relevant information from reading daily newspapers, the professional press, books and other literature and from listening to the radio and watching television. Although this vernacular professional learning is always taking place it is often overlooked in discussions about

INSET. It is too easy to be hooked on the course as the principal evidence of INSET activity.

In a similar vein it is possible to ignore the importance of the intense professional experience gained by those teachers who play active roles in professional associations of teachers and those secondary school teachers who engage in regular employment as question-setters and markers in examinations boards. This can be illustrated by the variety of experiences offered by a professional subject association. In a review (Williams 1988) of the INSET activities provided by the Geographical Association a list of twelve items was produced. These were:

1. Publication of two journals: *Teaching Geography* and *Geography*.
2. Publication of books and pamphlets.
3. Newsletters.
4. Local branch activity.
5. Annual conferences.
6. Regional conferences.
7. Section committees.
8. Working groups.
9. Working parties.
10. Validation of INSET Board.
11. Library and information services.
12. Links with cognate bodies.

For many geography teachers in England and Wales the journals published regularly by the Geographical Association (GA) provide important articles on the changing nature of the subject and communicate examples of classroom teaching and curriculum materials intended to assist in changing teachers' classroom behaviour. They give access to current debate about issues of direct relevance to geography specialists. Detailed reviews of textbooks, atlases, computer programs and other curriculum materials offer teachers professional guidance in the acquisition of resources for their teaching. In addition the GA commissions and publishes an array of books and pamphlets designed for a teacher readership. In recent years the list has been substantial, covering such issues as assessment, teaching pupils with special needs, geography and industry, integrated courses, departmental management, fieldwork and, more recently, aspects of the National Curriculum.

Several newsletters are prepared and distributed to specialist groups within the broad membership of the GA. An example is the LEA Advisers Newsletter, which is particularly important for promoting INSET for geography teachers, since it channels information about current developments in geography teaching and course organization to those LEA advisers who may lack relevant experience of geography teaching but who carry responsibility for this as part of a range of responsibilities within their LEAs.

Throughout England and Wales the GA has a network of more than 60 local branches run voluntarily by members, who are usually geography teachers from secondary schools. These branches arrange programmes of activities, including lectures, workshops, conferences, exhibitions, publications and field excursions. They constitute significant supplements or substitutes for INSET provided in geography by LEAs.

An important focal point for individual members and the branches is the Annual Conference of the GA held in London every Easter. Here issues of national importance are highlighted in a programme composed of keynote lectures, symposia, seminars and workshops given and led by national and international experts in the fields of geography and geographical education. In addition to the formal programme there is a major exhibition of commercially produced curriculum materials for geography teachers.

To administer the GA nationally, a number of section committees have been created to represent the interests of the principal phases of the education system – primary, secondary, further and higher. Parallel to these section committees are several working groups that have been established to bring together specialist interest groups, such as educational computing, environmental education, and new teaching techniques and methods. The section committees and the working groups arrange their own programmes of work and

139

have become a powerful mode of INSET for the participants. Not only do they learn through their collaborative activities, they also become a valuable resource for providing INSET activities at local and national levels. Their work is most obvious in the lists of GA publications and in the contributions made by group members to INSET courses, conferences, workshops and other activities.

The section committees and working groups are relatively permanent and differ from the short-lived working parties that are created to investigate and prepare reports on particular facets of geography in education. Working parties have been formed on such topics as examinations, integrated courses, multi-cultural education, careers, and geography and industry. Membership of these working parties is kept small and confined to enthusiasts drawn from various parts of England and Wales. They provide rich INSET experience for their members and for the GA members who gain the benefits of their work.

In 1983 the GA established a board to validate INSET courses. This was intended to give the Association's support to INSET activities that could be mounted in a variety of different venues, including teachers' centres, field study centres, schools and institutions of higher education. The board reflected a wish within the GA to improve the quality of INSET while, at the same time, providing a form of accreditation for short courses that was only available for long award-bearing courses in universities, polytechnics and colleges.

The library of the University of Sheffield houses the GA collection of publications, including a comprehensive school textbook collection. All GA members have access to this library.

Through the Great Debate, starting in 1976, and the intense consultative activity surrounding the introduction of the National Curriculum, the GA has pursued an active policy of collaboration with cognate bodies, including other subject associations, and preparation of authoritative statements written to ensure that the place of geography is properly recognized by important decision-makers. This collaboration has served to keep the membership of the GA well informed about contemporary issues and has provided activists with highly educational experiences.

This brief review of one subject association can be replicated for many other subject associations and other professional associations active in England and Wales. It is important to recognize that these associations count many thousands of teachers in their full membership and hundreds of teachers as active members at the heart of the activities arranged at local, regional and national levels. Yet many teachers would not regard these activities as INSET and many LEAs would not fund the activities of the activists from their INSET budgets.

Consultancies

The term consultancy has been widely used in the context of INSET, where it has become an umbrella to cover a wide range of different activities. For Golby and Fish (1980) a consultant is 'a provider who wishes to put himself at the disposal of a school in the interests of autonomous institutional and curriculum development'. It is the outsider role that is the most distinctive feature of the status of the consultant. He or she is brought into a situation in which a contribution can be made to the changing work of the school or classroom. However, a consultant can fulfil many roles and these may emerge at different times within the life of a single consultancy. Eraut (1977) started from this definition of a consultant: 'A consultant is any external agent from within the educational system who involves himself in discussing the educational problems of a class, department or school with a view to improving the quality of teaching and learning.'

Central to this operational definition is the distinction between the consultant and the client. There is an assumption that the external agent is invited by the teacher, as client, to engage in discussion to assist in the resolution of teacher-defined and school-based problems. As we shall see, consultancies can involve a great deal more than discussion, which is often important only in the initial stages of a developing consultant-

141

client relationship. Clarification of this relationship is offered by Golby and Fish (1980, p.84) in their list of clients in school-based consultancy work:

1. The sponsor: the agency providing finance and resources, normally an employing authority, but conceivably a publisher, project team or special interest group.
2. The initiator: where the first move came from, either internal to the school or external.
3. The headteacher: whose position relative to other clients is crucial.
4. Staff: involved directly in the consultancy.
5. Whole school staff: in so far as they are affected by the consultancy.
6. Pupils: those immediately and those potentially affected.
7. Parents: whether organized through a parent–teacher association or not.
8. Governors: whose interests are likely to increase in the post-Taylor era.
9. Local authority or employers: including both political members and professional officers, amongst whom will be those with a concern for in-service work.

Golby and Fish draw attention to the tension implicit in the differing expectations held by the various clients within any consultancy since each client brings a particular array of knowledge, experience and ability to the situation. Not surprisingly, given the variety of roles open to a consultant, the perception of different clients will vary according to the contexts in which they see the consultant at work. Thus pupils will see a classroom-based consultant through different eyes from the teacher who will differ in his or her perception from the headteacher who may have encountered the consultant only in the initial negotiating context. Eraut (1977) has provided a helpful typology of consultancy roles under eleven headings:

1. The expert.
2. Resource provider.
3. The promoter.
4. Career agent.
5. Link agent.
6. Inspector/evaluator.

7. Legitimator.
8. Ideas man.
9. Process helper.
10. Counsellor.
11. Change agent.

It is clear that there are many points of overlap between the roles. Distinguishing sharply between the expert, the promoter, the ideas man and the change agent is conceptually difficult both for a consultant and for a client. This is the value of such a loose word as consultant, since it permits a person to move between the roles without having to redefine the task that was identified as central in the initial stages of a consultancy arrangement.

Whether a consultant wishes it or not, he or she is a change agent. The direction, amount, intensity and duration of change may be highly variable and not sharply defined at the outset but there can be no doubt that some change, intended or unintended, will result from even a brief client–consultant association. It is here that Bolam's (1975) distinction between the change agent system, the innovatory system and the user system is helpful. As he asserts, these three systems begin as separate entities, then interact to bring about change and then separate. He goes on to argue that the most important basic characteristic of a change agent is the authority relationship that he or she has with the user system and this authority may be derived from administrative status, professional colleagueship, external consultancy or a combination of the three.

Some of the difficulties experienced by a consultant employed by an LEA as part of its TRIST programme have been identified in a study undertaken as part of an LEA's TRIST evaluation (Williams and England 1988). The LEA had appointed three full-time curriculum consultants and their specialisms were the world of work, microelectronics and technology, and active learning. The overall brief for each consultant was defined by the LEA and emphasized the need for teachers to develop new curriculum approaches and to examine their teaching methods, ultimately leading to teachers' adopting teaching styles that matched their curriculum content. For the active learning consultant the task was to address the following INSET needs: group work, pupils working in pairs, uses of pupil talk and writing for learning, active comprehension of written work, and simulation.

This consultant's target was the involvement of all the secondary school teachers in the LEA in active learning, particularly in matching curriculum content with appropriate classroom strategies for teaching and learning. To achieve this he began by using a change strategy that was empirical–rational (Chin and Benne 1969) in character. He started optimistically, believing that active learning could be easily understood by the teachers and others who were introduced to it. Experience of active learning techniques was gained in training sessions and the consultant assumed that the teachers would be able to adopt these in their classrooms quickly and easily. The feedback he gave to teachers who had participated in the training courses tended to be a summary of the curriculum and management issues, rather than of the active learning techniques. He learned that the teachers, although they had engaged in common training sessions, did not share a common understanding of the definition, principles and practice of active learning. He changed his training strategy to one that was more normative–re-educative. This strategy involved more than making the teachers aware of technically more effective ways of doing things. It involved changes in teachers' attitudes, values and norms, so that each teacher became a voluntary participant in the change process. The consultant focused more on providing examples of active learning techniques that characterized the training sessions and that could be adapted for use in classrooms. He also began to engage more in working alongside teachers in their classrooms.

Part of this consultant's task was convincing LEA advisers and deputy heads who were responsible for the curriculum that active learning was important for secondary school subject specialist teachers as well as for teachers who were responsible for personal and social education and class tutorials. The limiting of active learning to tutorial work and personal and social education was difficult to modify. What emerged, in the schools to which the consultant was invited to lead INSET days or to work with single subject departments, was piecemeal adoption of active learning strategies by some teachers in some lessons. Thus some teachers were introduced in INSET sessions to active learning techniques without obtaining an explanation of the significance of the techniques and without being encouraged to examine critically their own teaching styles. In other schools the techniques were introduced to teachers via consideration of non-academic areas, in the hope that these teachers would attempt to introduce them in their more usual subject teaching. However, it became clear that the individual teacher required considerable support if he or she was to sustain the new strategies. We (Williams and England 1988) concluded:

> The evaluation of this TRIST consultant's work has indicated that the following internal organizational changes are essential if progress in active learning is to be accomplished:
>
> 1. A participatory style of management of the school should be fostered to support staff during the period of personal uncertainty as they adapt to their changed teaching roles.
> 2. Opportunities should be made available for teachers to observe and to work with their peers who have already incorporated some active learning methods into their teaching.
> 3. Arrangements should be made to release all the staff of a particular functional group to examine together its current teaching methods and to receive introductory training in basic active learning teaching methods.

These conclusions are supported in the advice given in GRIDS handbooks, where the role of consultants has been considered in the light of the review of school policies. Consultants, whether they be LEA advisers, advisory teachers from an ESG project or staff from higher education, need to have their roles clearly defined through a process of negotiation, so that both teacher as client and consultant as stranger are clear about the objectives of a consultancy arrangement. Definition is also required regarding the method of working to be employed by the consultant within a specified timescale. It is evident in current INSET arrangements in England and Wales that consultancy is becoming increasingly popular. Consultants are introduced to schools sometimes working alone and sometimes as parts of advisory or project teams. The strength of the best consultancy arrangements lies in the tailor-made nature of the relationship. A good consultancy has clear objectives, is sufficiently flexible to accommodate easily to particular school circumstances and benefits from the expert knowledge and skills of a highly competent consultant. Where consultancies are less effective there has been a failure in the negotiation process, the consultant is insufficiently sensitive to the teachers' particular context and the consultant has not been adequately trained for the role.

INSET at a distance

Whereas a consultancy arrangement is commonly based on a one-to-one, face-to-face relationship between the consultant as trainer and the teacher, the distinguishing feature of distance learning arrangements is that there are intermediaries between the two. The intermediaries may be one or more different media – audio cassettes, video cassettes, radio and television broadcasts, books and other published materials – and there are a number of different arrangements whereby the teacher receives tutorial, counselling and assessment support from INSET providers.

Some of the most sophisticated and well-known INSET courses provided at a distance for teachers in Britain are the post-experience courses of the Open University. These courses are broadcast using television and radio channels and are supported by high quality books and tutorials. The expertise of the Open University was called upon to spearhead one of the major INSET initiatives in recent years, which was the preparation of secondary schoolteachers and others for the introduction of the General Certificate of Secondary Education (GCSE) examination. The programme of GCSE related INSET had two principal thrusts. First, there was the DES-funded national GCSE in-service training programme. Secondly, there was the programme of syllabus-specific INSET provided by the examinations boards.

The DES initiated its programme in 1985 with the publication of a statement, *General Certificate of Secondary Education: a general introduction* (Department of Education and Science/ Welsh Office 1985b), which was distributed to all schools and colleges. For secondary school specialists, the Secondary Examination Council commissioned the Open University to prepare and publish a number of subject-specific guides. These guides described the features of the new examination, paying close attention to the national criteria that were the foundations upon which the new examinations were based. Within the guides there were pages of factual information interspersed with activities designed to provoke the reader to react to the information provided. It was anticipated that the guides would be used by teachers and student teachers, who could read them in isolation or as part of a group. The guides were divided into sections designed for use in a series of INSET workshops or seminars. The authors were anxious to emphasize that the guides were intended to stimulate thought and discussion and were not intended to offer guidance relevant to a particular GCSE syllabus offered by any examinations board. It is important to notice that the guides could be seen as self-supported study materials, but using the videos produced by the Open University, it was possible for a teacher to work with the materials without the support of other teachers in an organized group setting.

Alongside the Open University materials and associated INSET activities there were training programmes offered by the examinations boards. The skeleton of the programme provided by one board was summarized in a circular published by the Northern Examining Association (NEA) in 1986. This emphasized that the NEA would be examining 99 GCSE syllabuses in 86 subjects in 1988. It stated that 'In most subjects opportunities will be provided for teachers to attend meetings at which the specific syllabus requirements will be discussed; in a very small number of subjects which do not involve major innovations, meetings will not be held but exemplar material may be made available.' The board arranged a number of one half-day or two half-day sessions related to particular subjects. Schools were each invited to send one teacher to these meetings, and it was to these arrangements that the expression 'cascade' was commonly applied, although the 'cascade' was much larger in scope than this. Essential to the training of teachers for the new examination was the need for each school to have individuals with a good understanding of the new examination in general; these individuals would have a training-of-trainers function in schools. In addition, for every subject there was a need to have a key individual who had received intensive training and who would have the responsibility for training colleagues from a particular subject in a school. For the purposes of the 'cascade' the NEA divided its subjects into categories and for each category there was a different training provision:

A: General meetings to discuss syllabus requirements.
B: Training in the conduct of particular forms of assessment.
C: Initial meetings to discuss syllabus requirements followed by a meeting later in the course for the purpose of standardizing or moderating.
D: Meetings for training, standardization or moderation.
E: No meetings but the provision of exemplar material.
F: No meetings or exemplar material.

Interesting light is thrown on this multi-faceted training programme in an evaluation report written by HMI (Her Majesty's Inspectorate 1988). The authors pointed to the essential ingredients of a cascade model for training, and these included the availability of expertise and the provision of training for the experts, the adequacy of links in the chain of dissemination from the centre to the periphery, the availability of well constructed training materials, the careful timing of the process, and the active involvement of senior staff from schools and members of the advisory staff in LEAs in the training programme. The GCSE cascade had a number of distinct phases in which distance learning for INSET was located.

The first phase opened in September 1985, when the GCSE Examining Groups set out to train trainers in two-day training events. In this phase, which focused on the principles and practice of the new examination, the Open University, with the British Broadcasting Corporation, made available distance learning materials comprising the videos and booklets referred to above. In the second phase, from January 1986, the trained experts commenced the training of subject specialists in schools and colleges and it was the responsibility of these trained specialists, in phase three (from February 1986), to train their subject colleagues in their own institutions. In phase three the responsibility for training passed to the LEAs. In the final phase, from September 1986, the Examining Groups provided training for teachers that was directly related to particular GCSE courses.

Through this phased operation it was intended to move from a consideration of the principles of the proposed examination through familiarization with national criteria for particular subjects and courses to a more detailed consideration of particular courses. The process was intended to be one of increasingly sharper focusing.

HMI pinpointed a number of defects in the GCSE cascade, including discontinuity in the phases, differences between teachers' expectations of provision and the actual provision, and weaknesses in the training-of-trainers provision. It is clear from the report that teachers wanted to by-pass the training concerned with general principles and move quickly to the actual subject syllabuses and subject-specific modes of assessment. Teachers wanted training materials to be more specific to their personal needs. 'Although the training guides were influential in setting the agenda for most INSET sessions and disseminating ideas about the types of exercises which could be used, their main value was in providing a framework within which many teachers devised their own materials and methods'

(HMI 1988). This comment has a general value in the consideration of distance learning in the context of INSET. Teachers wanted their training to be directly relevant to their own teaching contexts, i.e. the subjects they taught and the implications of the reformed examination for their own classes. This concern with the personalization of INSET is expressed in reviews and evaluations of distance learning treated more broadly (e.g. Harris 1987; Hodgson *et al.* 1987; Thorpe 1988).

The weaknesses of the GCSE cascade need to be placed alongside some of its strengths. For many teachers the training proved to be sufficient for them to introduce the new courses satisfactorily. It is impossible to gauge the reliance of teachers upon the training materials without the support of trained colleagues. It is also impossible to balance the impact of the training materials against the impact of the Examining Groups' syllabuses and sample examination papers.

It is interesting to note that the design of an INSET cascade has not been proposed for the introduction of the National Curriculum although training videos and a great variety of published materials have been made available by the DES, HMI, the National Curriculum Council (NCC), the School Examinations and Assessment Council (SEAC) and the Curriculum Council for Wales (CCW). The preparation of interim reports, consultation documents, framework documents, guidelines and non-statutory guidance documents has been followed by INSET training activities directly linked to the publications. These materials form the basis of distance learning for many teachers and their messages may be mediated by advisory teachers, advisers and others who assist in enabling teachers to relate the documents to their particular teaching contexts. As is acknowledged in the first issue of the *CCW Curriculum Bulletin*, published in October 1989, 'One of the main problems facing teachers these days is how to cope with the vast amount of literature dealing with the National Curriculum which is continuously pouring into schools.' One way of assisting teachers to cope with this is the establishment of a partnership between NERIS (the National Educational

Resources Information Service) and the two Curriculum
Councils (England and Wales). Using NERIS teachers are able to
have access to information on a database that is indexed to bring
out the links between different subjects, programmes of study,
attainment targets and a wide selection of teaching resources.

What was lacking from the GCSE cascade and is lacking
from the current dissemination and INSET activities associated
with the National Curriculum in England and Wales is a
general awareness of the potential of developments in tele-
communications for school-based and school-focused INSET. In
particular, there has been remarkably little experimentation in
INSET with teleconferencing. Teleconferencing is a generic term
for communication between individuals and groups at a distance
using some electronic device. There are four categories of
teleconferencing: audio teleconferencing, audiographic teleconferencing, video teleconferencing and computer teleconferencing.

Audio teleconferencing refers to interactive voice
communication between groups or individuals using
loudspeaking telephones, where the links between the
participants are provided through the telephone service with
links made possible by the use of an electronic bridge.
Audiographic teleconferencing makes use of the telephone
together with such equipment as the fax machine, electronic
blackboard and computers. In video teleconferencing the
emphasis is upon the use of one-way video through the
employment of television, with the interaction between
individuals or groups being provided by two-way telephone
communication. Computer conferencing can best be described
as an elaboration of electronic mail. The computer can be used
to provide graphic interactions in real time. Graphics and text
can be created and simultaneously transmitted to a variety of
locations. The INSET provider is able to produce original text
and graphics or provide images produced elsewhere and the
teacher can interact with the provider.

The items of equipment necessary for successful teleconferencing are becoming commonplace in educational institutions, but they have not received sufficient attention from

INSET providers and teachers. As more institutional clusters, consortia and networks are established and as teachers find it increasingly difficult to obtain release from their day-to-day teaching duties, the need to establish distance learning links for INSET becomes more important. Not only do such links have the potential to fill some of the gaps between teachers and INSET providers generally, they also provide the means of making a more effective use of scarce expertise in the INSET field. Building on the experience gained in INSET tele-conferencing in Australia, Canada, the USA and elsewhere, there is considerable scope for development in this field in Britain.

Action research as INSET

An important product of the work of the Schools Council was the emphasis given to grassroots curriculum development. The individual teacher was encouraged to experiment with new teaching approaches, to develop curriculum materials and to try out new methods of pupil assessment. The notion of the critical and reflective teacher working closely with colleagues inside and outside schools was an important feature of many of the projects supported by the Schools Council. The death of the Schools Council did not mark the end of curriculum develop-ment projects and national and local projects are currently being supported by a number of national agencies, including NCC, SEAC and the Training Agency. The need for teachers to be critical and reflective has become even greater as the balance between local and national curricular initiatives is being estab-lished. The use of the term 'action research' serves as a reminder that deliberate, conscious reflection is a vitally important component in the definition of a teacher.

Action research has become an international movement with teachers corresponding via regional and national networks and academics seeking to provide theoretical frameworks and consultancy support on which to base future progress. McKernan (1988) has provided a recent review of work in the field in which he identified sixteen key concepts in action research. His list embraced the motives for action research, its methodology and its products. The principal motive for the individual teacher is to improve the quality of his or her professional practice. Thus action research is undertaken by a teacher working alone, or collaboratively with colleagues inside or outside a school, on a problem or issue that is of immediate concern to the individual. Action research is based upon the study of an individual case and generally no attempt is made to control the variables relating to the matter being studied. Teachers as action researchers draw on a variety of research methods and the methodology may vary during the course of a particular study. There is considerable emphasis on the usefulness of the research; this usefulness is defined in terms of the needs of the individual teachers and the benefits gained by others who share the product.

Action research is commonly presented as a cyclical set of procedures that commence with the definition by a teacher of a problem situation. This is followed by the assessment of needs, the generation of hypotheses, the preparation of an action plan that is then implemented before evaluation and the specification of decisions. One cycle is perceived as leading to another and so the teacher gains professionally progressively through the cycles. For Carr and Kemmis (1986), an important part of this professional improvement is to be seen in the teacher as action researcher becoming more critical, interpretive and active. Although much weight is placed by advocates of action research on the autonomy of the teacher to define the problem situation, to select the appropriate research methods and to decide the audience for any findings considered worthy of dissemination, there is also discussion about the role of outsiders. In this discussion the role of consultants as facilitators and trusted friends has been considered. There is some overlap between the role of outsiders in action research and the role of INSET providers in the model for staff development described by Joyce and Showers (1980). In this model coaching teams are set up to assist teachers to follow a sequence of training events, summarized as: theory – demonstration – practice – feedback –

follow-up. This sequence is intended to provide opportunities for training sessions, experimentation with new practices, classroom observation of teaching and the exchange of teacher experience.

The action research movement has attracted many teachers, although they represent only a small minority of the total teaching force. The strength of the movement lies in alerting teachers to their capacity for self-improvement. For the busy teacher familiar with the principles underpinning action research, the principal difficulty is making the deliberate commitment to follow a formal research programme that will not interfere with other aspects of the teaching role. All teachers are likely to argue that they are always engaged in making evaluative judgements about their work and that they are constantly seeking to improve their performance as teachers. Crossing the threshold of making deliberate, conscious efforts to be a researcher is a difficult step, made more difficult if there is no support structure available inside or outside the school.

In this chapter various ways have been described by which teachers can gain INSET experiences without having to set aside their day-by-day teaching. It is important for teachers, heads of schools, INSET co-ordinators in schools and LEAs, and INSET providers to pay close attention to these alternatives to courses. Too often the provision of courses, conferences and workshops is considered to be the only way of providing teachers with training. Paying increasing attention to alternatives to courses should result in more teachers gaining the benefits of INSET.

7 Evaluation

Much lip-service has been paid to the evaluation of INSET. No one would disagree that it was necessary, although there is a substantial distance between espousal of the principles underpinning good practice and the practice itself. Much, of course, depends on the scale of the INSET activity and the precise function of any evaluation exercise. Acknowledging that most INSET is ultimately concerned with improving the educational opportunities and experiences of children and young people in classrooms, we would expect most evaluation to focus on classrooms; the appropriate location for INSET evaluation would be the classroom. Yet this is not commonly the case. This does not overlook or deny the importance of teacher self-evaluation, but the addition of the word 'self' to evaluation changes the perspective markedly. In this chapter I shall describe and comment on a number of recently published evaluation studies before discussing some of the principles upon which the practice of INSET evaluation is grounded.

The evaluation of TRIST

For the evaluation of TRIST the Manpower Services Commission set up three projects. These were additional to the requirement that each LEA should make its own INSET evaluation arrangements. There was a national evaluation, a study of local evaluations and a meta-evaluation study.

The national evaluation
This study was undertaken by a project team comprising two co-

ordinators, one full-time researcher and three part-time researchers, based at the University of Surrey and the Roehampton Institute of Education. The project had these terms of reference: 'To assess the extent to which TRIST is promoting more systematic approaches to INSET planning and delivery across the curriculum of the kind envisaged by the principles of TVEI in the education and training of teachers.'

The project report (Battle *et al.* 1988) has 77 pages and the second chapter describes the research design and methodology. It is recorded that the intended users of the evaluation report were the MSC, the DES and LEAs and their institutions. While the MSC required a summative report on TRIST, it was assumed that the LEAs would require formative data that would be useful to them in the longer term development of effective models for the management and delivery of INSET.

The main questions addressed in the study were:

- What are the main changes in INSET provision resulting from TRIST?
- What models of management, delivery and content are found within TRIST schemes?
- What relationships exist between LEA context and INSET developments under TRIST?
- What are the key elements of the strategies used?
- What helped or hindered the change process?
- What lessons can be drawn from the TRIST experience to inform post-TRIST INSET management and delivery?
- How has TRIST specifically informed new INSET arrangements?

To answer these questions a two-stage evaluation strategy was designed with the guidance of an MSC committee drawing its membership from the MSC (TVEI and TRIST), the DES and HMI.

Stage 1 extended from April to September 1986 and stage 2 followed from September 1986 to April 1987. The authors of the report record for stage 1 that the brief was 'to identify and analyse models of TRIST, with particular reference to models of management and delivery and to overall LEA goals'. For stage 2, the brief was 'to undertake sample surveys and case studies in selected LEAs, in order to illuminate practices in the management and delivery of INSET.'

Underlying the evaluation strategy were four assumptions. First, there was the need for flexibility to accommodate the diversity and change encompassed in the TRIST programme. Secondly, the interim, short-term nature of TRIST, which encouraged LEAs to establish arrangements that would continue and develop after TRIST terminated, had to be recognized. Thirdly, there was a need to avoid duplication between local evaluation and national evaluation studies. Fourthly, there were limits of scale and scope imposed by resources availability, the pressures from the funding body and the targets for the evaluation.

In the first stage of the study, LEA consolidated plans and termly monitoring reports were made available by MSC for

	TYPE 1	TYPE 2	TYPE 3
A. Policy appraisal and formulation; Identification of needs and opportunities. Goal setting and planning.	Top down Ad hoc/'Bolt on' Centralist Few key individuals	Bottom up (or bottom only) Segregated	Integrated Pluralist Many 'key' individuals/groups
B. Organizational Structure/Strategy Channels of Communication (Management Structure)	Hierarchical, Vertical communication Formal Competitive	Autonomous Self-contained Informal	Democratic Vertical and horizontal communication. Formal and informal networks Cooperative/coalition
C. Financial Control. Budgeting/Costing Monitoring of spending Authorization of spending	Centralized — with minimum delegation. Broad 'implicit' definitions	Mainly devolved to locality, individual. In-house 'specific' definitions	Mostly devolved — maximum delegation with overview at centre. Negotiated 'explicit' definitions and control mechanisms.
D. Evaluation — strategic — local (Quality Control)	Ad hoc, uncoordinated Evaluation, from top or by external agency.	Self and/or Peer evaluation	At all levels Built into system Continuous and cyclical Internal and external

TIME DIMENSIONS→INITIAL PLAN→CONSOLIDATED PLAN→IMPLEMENTATION → RESIDUE/LEGACY

Figure 7.1   Typology of INSET management – TRIST.

157

Outcome/Goal of the Training	Focus of the training			
	Curriculum Development (1) a) b)	Professional Development (2) a) b)	Institutional Development (3) a) b)	LEA Development (4)
Individual Teacher with updated skills				
Tutor/Trainer				
Team Leader/ Team Builder				

1. Curriculum Development: a) Specific subjects or skills, b) Cross-curriculum themes
2. Professional Development: a) Subject knowledge, b) Teaching and organizational skills
3. Institutional Development: a) School or college focus, b) Consortia or institutional networks
4. LEA Development: Training for Advisers, INSET Co-ordinator or Managers, Officers etc.

Figure 7.2   Typology for the content of TRIST training
              programmes.

reading and analysis. This documentation study was enhanced
by discussions with selected LEA personnel, who provided
information about 'how the plans related to LEA goals, what
models and strategies were being used for achieving change, and
how the plans were unfolding'. From this it was possible to
construct three typologies of models which focused on INSET
management, content and delivery. These typologies are
illustrated in Figure 7.1 (management), Figure 7.2 (content) and
Figure 7.3 (delivery), which were included in the evaluation
report.

    In the second stage, fifteen LEAs were selected for detailed
study. The intention was 'to gather information which would
allow some evaluation judgements to be made regarding the
degree of change occurring in the organisation and management
of TRIST when compared with the LEA's normal INSET

management, and also to illuminate practices occurring in management and delivery in TRIST schemes'.

In selecting the LEAs, attention was paid to geographical spread across England and Wales, to the regional structure used by MSC for administration and management, and to variations in LEA characteristics such as size, type of authority, structure, political control and local economy. There were also educational considerations, such as the number of schools and colleges, the number of pupils attending secondary schools and the number of 16–18-year-olds in further education, the TRIST

Location of Training	Identity of Trainer		
	Central Provider (HE Lecturer)	LEA (Adviser)	School/College (Teacher)
External — HE institution, industry or distance learning		(a) individual (b) team	(a) individual (b) team
Internal (i) Local Authority — teachers' centre or staff training college			
Internal (ii) Institution — college-based, school-based, classroom			

Figure 7.3   Typology of TRIST delivery.

funding bands, the participation of LEAs in TVEI and the size of advisory services. Attention was also paid to the three typologies drawn up in stage 1. Access to the identified LEAs was negotiated and guidelines, which included ethical considerations with particular reference to confidentiality, were prepared for the researchers.

The focus in stage 2 was on the management and delivery of TRIST and its impact on INSET in the LEAs over time. TRIST regional advisers and regional managers were interviewed to provide contextual information about LEAs and the MSC regions in which they were located. For the selected LEAs the TRIST co-ordinators, evaluators and INSET advisers were interviewed using semi-structured interview schedules. These in-depth interviews were supplemented by shorter interviews with persons drawn from the teaching profession, LEA officers and administrators, 'outsiders' (higher education INSET providers and industry representatives) and lay persons. Not all these groups were represented in every interview programme.

A further dimension of the study was the preparation of a number of case-studies of training activities, which sought to provide insights into the contextual nature of development, the acceleration of development through specific funding, innovative strategies, and the management of planned and focused initiatives in INSET.

> The team concentrated on studies illuminating one LEA's approach to the systematic evaluation of INSET needs, another LEA's approach to the use of cross-Authority teams as a change strategy in one of their designated priority areas – assertiveness training for women teachers; one school's approach to staff development in TVEI; an LEA-wide initiative in industry–education links illustrating design issues in active learning strategies; and one LEA's approach to the development of cross-curricular teams involving Advisers and teachers from different schools. (Battle *et al.* 1988, p. 14)

From these case-studies the research team was able to describe a number of key features of the TRIST scheme, including: identification of training need procedures; cross-institutional collaboration; the use of teacher expertise; the training of trainers; and different evaluation and dissemination strategies. Within the case-studies a number of different research methods were employed. Reference is made in the report to participant observation, interviewing, documentation studies and participation and observation at meetings. Throughout, the emphasis was upon the collection of qualitative data. The difficulties of making generalizations from the small sample of LEAs are reported. The research team adopted the use of the adjectives 'few', 'some' or 'many' to indicate the numbers involved: a 'few' referred to less than one-third of the fifteen LEAs, 'some' to one-third to two-thirds and 'many' to more than two-thirds.

This study is clearly concerned with infrastructural issues relating to the introduction of a short-lived management innovation. For the evaluators the principal task was to try to capture the local character of the responses to the TRIST initiative while seeking to gain insights and understandings that were worthy of the attention of persons interested in INSET across the country and that would have a formative role in influencing the organization and management of INSET once the TRIST funding had ceased. The timescale was remarkably short – five school terms – and funding was insufficient to enable the evaluators either to undertake studies of LEA practices before the introduction of TRIST or to follow the selected LEAs and interviewed personnel once TRIST funding had ended. With regard to the evaluation methodology, the interest lies in the eclectic approach, the pragmatic design and the balance between detailed case-studies and a more general study. As was indicated earlier, this study was one of three evaluation studies commissioned under TRIST; the second focused on dissemination.

The DELTA project

The DELTA project was undertaken at the Cambridge Institute of Education by a team of three, which included two seconded teachers and an institute tutor. The team produced a report (Holly *et al.* 1987) of 61 pages in which they describe how they sought to achieve their aims and their findings. DELTA is an acronym for Dissemination arising from Evaluations of Local TRIST Activities. The aims of the project were:

- To synthesize the findings of local evaluations of TRIST.
- To do so by means of a participant dialogue at regional workshops, thereby making the dissemination itself an active learning experience.
- To complement, and liaise with, the other elements within the MSC's dissemination package.

To achieve these aims a four-step programme was undertaken. In the first step workshops were arranged as the central component of an interactive process that was designed to enable participants in TRIST at all levels to share their experiences and perceptions gained from involvement in the scheme. Evidence from the workshops provided the 'grounded framework', which was substantiated and authenticated by the local evaluation reports studied in the second step. In the third step the synthesis achieved in step 2 was examined with some degree of objectivity in terms of processes and products. In the final step the findings were disseminated with recommendations.

The authors of the report assert that their research rested on six 'evaluation dimensions', which aimed to:

- Promote local experience at the national level.
- Give the internal knowledge an external platform.
- Provide a summative account of the formative, developmental processes generated during the life of TRIST.
- Render the particular general, and the subjective objective.
- Emphasize the value of both products and processes.
- Provide empirical evidence of the intrinsic qualities of TRIST activities.

The substance of their findings is presented in the report under four headings: establishing INSET; applying INSET; supporting INSET; and evaluating INSET. Under each heading there appear a number of brief general statements enhanced by quotations derived from the workshops and from local TRIST documents.

The meta-evaluation study

This third component of the national evaluation of TRIST was undertaken at the University of Sussex by a team of three led by Professor Michael Eraut. As its title suggests, this was a study of the evaluation processes relevant to TRIST within LEAs. The original objectives of the study were spelled out in the final report (Eraut *et al.* 1988):

1. To describe and analyse the range of evaluation practice in one TRIST region, South Thames.
2. To supplement this analysis with accounts of a small number of local evaluations in other regions (chosen because they differ in some significant way from those within South Thames).
3. To assess the costs of these evaluations in order to provide a clearer idea of what can be obtained for a given financial commitment.
4. To examine factors which affect the selection and implementation of evaluation methods, e.g. cost, scope, expectations of LEA, institutional base of evaluator, prior training and experience of evaluator.
5. To ascertain what kinds of information evaluators are seeking to provide, in what form and for whom.
6. To seek evidence of the effects of evaluation while they are still in progress, both intended (through informal communications and interim reports) and unintended (the investigator effect).
7. To ascertain whether and in what ways TRIST had been influenced by evidence from TRIST evaluations.
8. To make recommendations about the role, conduct and financing of local evaluations.

Of these eight aims, the seventh was abandoned and the others were met to varying degrees through a research programme that took in the thirteen LEAs in the South Thames region plus three selected from other parts of the country. Interviews were conducted with TRIST co-ordinators, evaluators and inspectors/advisers, and with officers with responsibility for TRIST. Documentation analysis and respondent verification were other research methods employed. For documentation analysis the researchers had access to LEA TRIST submissions, evaluation instruments and a number of evaluation reports. Respondent verification took the form of submitting two interim meta-evaluation reports to each informant and informal discussion of the reports in a project steering committee. Finally, questionnaires were distributed to participants in two national conferences called to discuss the impact of TRIST; these sought guidance on the issues that ought to be addressed in the final report.

The findings of the study were presented in a 67 page report under four main headings: What is evaluation and who does it?; The management of evaluation; Evaluating INSET courses and activities; and Strategic evaluation. The list of recommendations is of particular relevance for this chapter, since it provides a checklist for LEAs and local INSET evaluators against which to monitor their progress since TRIST:

1. Local evaluations of INSET programmes should ideally include both internal and external elements.
2. Internal evaluators need good training in evaluation.
3. Wherever possible, secondment for evaluation should be made on a full-time basis.
4. Training should be provided in the management of evaluation.
5. Training in professional monitoring should be considered for inspectors, advisers, advisory teachers and school INSET co-ordinators, with particular attention to their roles in INSET evaluation.
6. The costs of professional monitoring should be borne by the relevant INSET courses and activities, not charged to the evaluation budget.
7. Professional monitoring of courses should be standard practice for all providers.
8. An evaluation should have a clear initial brief.
9. Each authority should establish a small committee or advisory group for INSET evaluation.
10. The flow of information from professional monitoring of INSET should be co-ordinated and linked with the work of designated evaluators and their committees.
11. Codes of practice for evaluating evaluation data should be established and observed.
12. Procedures for reporting and feedback should be discussed during

the early stages of an evaluation, to give guidance to evaluators and to ensure maximum utilization of their findings.

13. Evaluators should seek multiple sources of evidence to 'triangulate' their findings.

14. Evaluators should elicit questions from stakeholders and negotiate which of them should be addressed, in what form and with what criteria in mind.

15. Evaluations assessing the effectiveness of INSET activities should take into account differences in expectation, preparation and follow-up, and the school and classroom contexts of participants.

16. From an LEA standpoint, INSET evaluation should focus on the link between INSET and teacher attitudes and behaviour, while school-based evaluation should focus on the link between school policy and practice and pupils' attitudes and achievements.

17. From a school or college standpoint, INSET evaluation should assess the match between INSET provision and the curriculum and staff development needs which they themselves have identified.

18. INSET evaluations should give more attention to strategic questions and policy issues that are relevant to several programmes or to general patterns of INSET management and delivery.

19. Evaluations should consider INSET programmes as appropriate targets for professional review, so that the combined effect of INSET activities can be examined in a coherent way.

20. Strategic evaluation of INSET policies and programmes should re-examine their assumptions about INSET needs.

21. The needs assessment process is so critical at both LEA and institutional levels that it should also be reviewed during INSET evaluation.

The evaluation of Project Impact

Project Impact was a DES-funded project undertaken from 1983 to 1986 jointly by Huddersfield Polytechnic, the Hester Adrian Research Centre and the Department of Education at the University of Manchester (Robson *et al.* 1988). It had three parts and the one that is of interest in the context of INSET evaluation was concerned with the development and evaluation of short courses. Six school-focused short courses in special education were selected for study. Each course was approximately 30 contact hours in duration. As part of the project, assistance was given by the project team to the course organizers in the design of the courses and the preparation of course materials. The courses were repeated several times and, in their initial presentation, pilot evaluation studies were conducted, which resulted in changes to the course materials, organization, presentation and evaluation of the courses.

The total evaluation programme comprised six pilot studies and four field studies. For each course the evaluation strategy remained the same: 'to obtain extensive questionnaire data from all the participants and to supplement this with additional observational and interview data from a subgroup of teachers participating in the course' (Robson *et al.* 1988). A clear description of the methods used in short-course evaluation in the project is given here:

1. Pre-course interviews of a subset of intending participants.
2. Participants' perceptions and current practice sheet. All participants were asked to complete a sheet on registration for the course at the beginning of the week. This covered the reasons for attending the course, their views of the course objectives and aspects of their current practice.
3. Content evaluation sheets. At the first session of the course all participants were given a content evaluation sheet and were asked to complete this after each session during the week. This covered their ratings of the usefulness and interest of the sessions, their expectations about whether or not the session would change their approach in school and gave an invitation to comment more generally.
4. During-course interviews. A subset of course participants, including those interviewed prior to the course, were also interviewed towards the end of the course to obtain their views on how the course was progressing. They were also invited to comment on the evaluation itself.
5. Information sheets. Halfway through the course participants were asked to complete the standard Project Impact information sheet giving details of their background and experience.
6. Participants' perceptions and future plans sheet. At the end of the course participants were invited to give their views on the contribution of the microcomputer to their work, their present view

of the course objectives, what they would do differently in school as a result of the course and also to comment on various general aspects of the course.

7. Follow-up sheet. All participants were asked to complete a follow-up sheet approximately three months after completion of the course concentrating on ways in which the course has affected their practice.

8. Follow-up interviews. On receipt of completed follow-up sheets a subset of participants were interviewed and/or observed in school.

This list demonstrates that short-course evaluation is a multi-stage process that begins with course preparation, continues through the course and ends in the follow-up stage. A number of discrete, though interrelated, stages can be identified as a theoretical structure for the evaluation of a training course:

1. Evaluation of the pre-course context.
2. Evaluation of the preparation of the participants.
3. Evaluation of the preparation of the providers.
4. Evaluation of the immediate pre-course context.
5. Evaluation of the course in action.
6. Evaluation of the immediate post-course context ('happy hour' evaluation).
7. Evaluation of the follow-up of the participants.
8. Evaluation of the follow-up of the providers.
9. Evaluation of the post-course context.

It is rare to find that time and other resources are available for INSET evaluators to undertake such a thorough and comprehensive evaluation of a course.

Short-course evaluation

In order to provide more detailed information on the evaluation of short courses I have chosen a number of published evaluation studies. The first of these is concerned with the planning of an INSET course.

Planning an INSET course

Bell (1980) describes an evaluation study that sought to identify the perceptions, assumptions and intentions of the organizers of an INSET course on educational management for middle school headteachers. He records the discussions that took place between LEA and university representatives in the planning stage. As he states: 'Notions about the nature of management in middle schools, the roles which ought to be played by the headteacher and assumptions about middle schools themselves were all inherent in the planning of this course.' He describes some of these notions and argues that the key areas of content of the course rested on assumptions about the nature of middle schools and the extent to which they should become places in which specialist teaching occurs. The product of the planning process was a course profile. 'Decisions which were consciously taken and important factors which were never the result of any conscious attempt at decision making have combined to provide a profile for this course which, whilst perhaps not always explicit in the minds of the course organizers, were [sic] nevertheless crucial in determining the way in which the course was received by those middle school headteachers who attended it.' The principal features of this profile are summarized in Figure 7.4.

The value of this profile is that it provides criteria for evaluating the planning stage. These are expressed in the principal headings: general organization, change strategy, formulation process, etc. In the middle column are the conclusions reached in discussion by the planners; the final column indicates alternative courses of action that they might have followed. Care must be taken in reading these two columns. Bell identifies three difficulties associated with them. First, the implication may be drawn from the listing of the items in the columns that each column has an internal consistency. Bell writes: 'It might be assumed that any course with a solution-based general orientation must also have knowledge presented by experts in a rigid course structure with a mode of teaching which is teacher rather than learner centred.' This is clearly inconsistent. Secondly, looking across the items in the columns, they are not mutually exclusive. The columns are intended simply to illustrate the overall tendency in each case. Thirdly,

GENERAL ORGANIZATION:	Solution	Not problem
CHANGE STRATEGY:	Implicit	Not explicit

FORMULATION PROCESS:

i. Planning	Closed	Not open
ii. Participation	Minimized	Not maximized
iii. Control	LEA	Not headteachers
iv. Knowledge	Expert	Not common sense

STRUCTURE OF COURSE:

i. Duration	Short	Not long
ii. Organization	Rigid	Not flexible
iii. Target	Individual	Not group

CONTENT OF COURSE:

i. Access	Restricted	Not free
ii. Presentation	Practical	Not theoretical
iii. Emphasis	Teacher	Not learner
iv. Focus	Educational	Not management

CONTROL OF COURSE:	LEA	Not course members

Figure 7.4   Profile summary.

the profile needs to be considered in a time dimension, since the significance of different aspects is likely to vary over the life of a course. Despite these limitations the profile has interest for teachers, providers and planners concerned with INSET. It reminds us that even in those early meetings convened to discuss INSET provision, when no precise agenda is on the table, a number of central issues emerge that can be categorized by an external evaluator or a participant observer. The items that appear in each category indicate the assumptions, expectations and intentions of the planners. These clearly colour the course or other activity that may eventually be provided. An evaluator following the life of an INSET course from planning stage to completion would find the construction of a course profile, based on the initial discussions, a useful basis on which to negotiate the target for evaluation. This gives any INSET course evaluation a sharp focus and gives the evaluator guidance in selecting the appropriate evaluation strategy and methods.

Presenting a course

The DES sponsored the Colleges Curriculum Project, which was conducted by the University of Leeds School of Education and the National Foundation of Educational Research. As part of the work of this project an evaluation study, reported by Hoste (1977), was made of a one-term in-service course for teachers of reading that was based on an Open University post-experience course. Hoste asserts: 'In evaluation, the evidence available is . . . capable of alternative explanation, surrounded by margins of error, approximate and hedged with speculation. But the more mutually independent sources which can be tapped to provide information, the more likely it is that we shall be able to come to some fairly positive conclusions about our courses.' He goes on to describe an evaluation strategy that included a blend of techniques, including participant observation, interview, discussion, semantic differential rating scales and a post-course questionnaire.

The evaluator attended course sessions in which he participated and recorded 'notes of the main trends, especially any which seemed to him to raise particular problems for tutors or students'. He also tape-recorded a discussion between course attenders and the tutors, which identified a number of related areas described in an evaluation report given to the tutors. He commented that this almost totally unobtrusive data-collecting technique provided a considerable amount of information that could be sifted at leisure, leading to the compilation of a document that could be used as the basis for comparison between courses and as one part of the on-going evaluation of the reading course that was the focus of the study. Information about the interviews and post-course questionnaires was not provided in Hoste's published paper but he did give details about the semantic differential scales he developed. These scales had been validated in a variety of contexts in teacher education as part of the work of the project. An example of one of the scales is shown in Figure 7.5.

The expression 'happy hour evaluation' is used, often disparagingly, to describe the collection from course attenders of their impressions of a course unit or a whole course immediately after its completion. Hoste's semantic differential scale is the kind of instrument that can be administered quickly and can obtain responses from participants without requiring them to give up time and energy when they are probably anxious to leave a course venue. It provides a range of descriptors that individually are open to various kinds of interpretation but that nevertheless yield patterns to serve as the basis for comparison and as formative guidance for course planners and providers. As the course tutors (Cooper and Sellors 1977) commented, 'A single profile has little meaning; it acquires significance, however, by comparison with others for the course, or parts of the course, for which the same tutors are responsible.'

Useful	Useless
Bad	Good
Easy	Difficult
Enjoyable	Detestable
Fragmented	Coherent
Satisfying	Disappointing
Confusing	Clear
Worthless	Valuable
Vital	Unnecessary
Narrow	Wide
Consistent	Variable
Optimistic	Pessimistic
False	True
Relevant	Irrelevant
Weak	Strong
Deep	Shallow
Passive	Active
Small	Large
Informative	Uninformative
Practical	Theoretical
Boring	Interesting
Fast	Slow
Formal	Informal
Imaginative	Conventional
Uninspiring	Stimulating

Figure 7.5   Hoste's semantic differential profile.

It is worth reflecting on the difference between this kind of instrument and the evaluation report forms often used by schools. It is not unusual to find teachers being expected to complete a form, such as that reproduced in Figure 7.6, which is used by a comprehensive secondary school, on their return to school at the end of an INSET course. Notice that this form has the purposes of routeing the experiences gained from course attendance into the appropriate part of the school and providing guidance for future staff development activities. It also asks the teacher to make a judgement on the benefits that he or she has gained through attending a course. It has a formative function, both for the individual teacher and for the school. It does not contribute to the providers' future organization of a course.

Follow-up to a course

Once course attendance has been completed it is usually difficult for teachers to receive any follow-up support, guidance or assistance from INSET providers. This is especially true in those circumstances where course attenders are numerous, where they come from widely scattered schools and where the course was provided by an organization or individual not closely involved with teachers, schools or LEAs. Sometimes it is possible for a course group to reconvene for refresher purposes and sometimes, for LEA provided courses, advisers, advisory teachers and other support staff may be able to visit teachers in their schools to offer them course-related support. The word 'support' is not easily defined, since it can encompass everything from casual conversations in school corridors through the provision of resource materials to the provision of a consultant who assists a teacher in day-to-day work in a classroom.

An interesting evaluation study of the follow-up to an INSET course for Australian school principals was reported by Sadler (1984). More than 200 primary school principals (headteachers) took part in an action research programme called 'Principals for Change'. They came from twelve districts in Queensland and in each district two rounds of workshops were held, each separated by about ten weeks. Between the workshops the principals were

A. Teacher's name ....

B. Course subject/title ....
....

C. Organizing body/person/institution |..
....

D. Date ....

E. Why was the course chosen? ....
....
....
....

F. Please answer the following questions after you have attended the course:

   1. Did the course:

               meet your expectations .... YES   NO
               benefit you personally .... YES   NO
               benefit your departmental work .... YES   NO
               benefit your pastoral work .... YES   NO
               provide useful input on whole
               school or cross-curricular issues .... YES   NO

     Comments: ....
....
....
....
....

   2. Actions to be taken or recommended (please tick as appropriate):

               Report back to departmental/team meeting
               Feedback through head of year
               Report to head
               Informal feedback to interested staff
               Report back to cross-curricular team
               Issue for senior management team to discuss
               Issue for deputy head action
               Issue for middle management team to discuss
               Issue for staff meeting
               Recommended as a topic for a staff development day
               No action recommended/needed

   3. Do you feel that any of the speakers/lecturers/course leaders could provide useful input for a school staff development day?

   Name(s)   Topic(s)   Place of Contact
  ....

Figure 7.6   INSET evaluation report.

expected to produce an action plan to be implemented, developed and refined in their schools. They returned for a second round of workshops, which were designed for collaborative reflection on their experience in order that general principles and techniques for bringing about change could be identified and reinforced. The programme was evaluated by an external evaluator and a follow-up evaluation was conducted by two evaluators a year after the workshops had been completed. This follow-up evaluation was designed to assess the long-term effects of the INSET programme at school level. The evaluation strategy was based on a pilot questionnaire, a main survey questionnaire and interviews with 30 of the workshop attenders.

Sadler comments, 'Follow-up evaluation appears simple in principle, the aim being to obtain a global assessment of impact by taking a snapshot some time after a programme finishes . . . The timing of the evaluation, the extent and nature of support services, and the reactivity of the evaluation all act to complicate follow-up evaluation.' The evidence from the follow-up study indicated the variety of 'activity levels' of the principals that resulted from the workshops. The evaluators reported that a receptive attitude to change and a willingness to engage in change were insufficient. There was also a need for periodic 'topping up, or at least some external moral support'. It was emphasized that 'for professional development programmes, the general design problem is not merely devising a satisfactory plan for achieving a good initial result, but working out how to allocate resources across the original programme *and for subsequent refreshment,* and how best to provide the latter, so that the total impact is maximized.' They commented that even the filling in of the evaluation questionnaire or being interviewed served to rekindle interest in the development programme. The principals suggested four different strategies for follow-up: a series of informal meetings of principals; the redesign of the workshop programme as a joint activity between principals and their teachers; consolidation through a second involvement in the programme; and consolidation through extension in the form of a supplementary programme.

In a review of the evaluation methodology, Sadler reflects on the inadequacies of the pilot questionnaires completed by one sample of principals who had participated in the programme, and another sample from non-participant principals. A significant finding in the course of the interviews was the dissatisfaction expressed by some principals with the non-receipt of feedback from the evaluation conducted during the workshops.

General principles underlying evaluation

The evaluation of INSET has received increasing attention as the annual cycle of planning and implementing INSET in LEAs has become a normal procedure. So far in this chapter I have described evaluation studies conducted in the context largely of special projects. The evaluation techniques employed, like the projects with which they were associated, were developed in the light of the particular contexts of the projects. This response to context is an important consideration, since it draws attention to the lack of hard and fast guidelines for LEAs, schools and teachers wishing to engage in evaluation.

The DES were sufficiently concerned about the monitoring and evaluation of INSET to produce in 1987 a note of guidance directed at LEAs and, in particular, at INSET co-ordinators. The note was supplemented by conferences at which the matter of INSET evaluation within LEAs was discussed. The note (DES 1987) addressed five major questions:

i. who will use the results of monitoring and evaluation?
ii. for what purposes will they be used?
iii. what should be monitored and evaluated?
iv. how should the monitoring and evaluation be carried out?
v. who should carry out the evaluation and monitoring?

Given the emphasis on funding within LEATGS it is not surprising to find that the preferred definition of evaluation in the note focuses on the 'value of the outcomes, positive and negative'. In an early discussion about the nature of evaluation,

Cronbach (1963) drew attention to the distinction between 'the collection and use of information to make decisions about an educational program'. The terms 'monitoring' and 'evaluation' help to clarify the distinction between data collection and the description of particular features of an INSET activity and the bringing of judgement to bear on that activity. There is an important difference between the evaluator who gathers information and presents it in a non-judgemental way and the evaluator who gathers information and makes judgements about the quality of the information that has been gathered. Nevo (1986) has drawn attention to this difference in his attempt to define evaluation. He reports the conclusion of a joint committee on standards for evaluation in the USA, which defined evaluation as 'the systematic investigation of the worth or merit of some object' (Joint Committee 1981) and draws attention to the alternative view of Cronbach and his associates (1980), who advocate a non-judgemental position.

As is asserted in the DES list, the findings of any evaluation will be useful to someone. They should facilitate improved decision-making by INSET planners and providers. They should also help teachers who have participated in INSET activities and thus improve the educational experiences of pupils and students. In the context of LEATGS, the DES identifies three main uses for evaluation information: to underpin the identification of training needs; to improve training and the systems by which it is planned, managed, implemented and followed up; and to render the participants in the scheme accountable. This identification of uses leads to a systems focus, since it is at the level of the LEA planning system that the DES note is directed. It is made clear that the detailed planning and provision of particular training activities is not the concern of the DES. This is a matter for LEAs and for schools.

At a systems level LEAs are encouraged by the DES to devise a rolling programme that would enable them to focus on particular features of their INSET planning and provision. Such a rolling programme should take account of infrastructural considerations as well as provision. It should include the arrangements made within the LEA for establishing the appropriate structures for linking the LEA with the schools and for enabling schools to collaborate as consortia, pyramids or clusters. It should pay close attention to needs identification arrangements, since upon the effectiveness of these arrangements rests the quality and quantity of the INSET provision. Ways by which needs are prioritized and associated INSET activities are planned require careful evaluation. All these evaluation studies are at the systems level. The balance between LEA provided INSET, through, for example, the use of teachers' centres, the employment of advisory teachers and the arrangement of residential conferences, and school planned and provided INSET is a crucial consideration. The balance between INSET activities that meet the personal needs of the individual teacher and those that are more directly concerned with the needs of the whole school and the LEA is also important. In this regard, attention should be paid to the implications for schools of the shift away from the pattern of full-time and part-time secondment of teachers to take up teacher fellowships or to attend award-bearing courses, and the move towards short, often one-day, events directed at large numbers of teachers.

The DES note acknowledges the difficulties likely to be encountered by LEAs that seek to gather detailed information about training activities. 'The LEA's central administration of training generally has no need or capacity to act on the information, besides risking being overwhelmed by the bulk of the material. But it may need to see a sample of such evaluations, for purposes such as monitoring and evaluating the management systems or the effectiveness of training, and accountability.' Crucial is the assertion in the note that 'no training experience should be undertaken without an evaluation of its effects in relation to the needs originally perceived'.

What emerges from the DES note is the distinction at LEA and school levels between the evaluation of strategic matters and of logistical matters. Evaluation data related to single training events or particular aspects of INSET management must be brought together to inform decision-makers at the strategy-determining level. As has been discussed in earlier chapters, there is a need for strategic INSET planning at DES, LEA, school and functional group levels and, because of the nature of INSET funding, it is essential for the levels to be working harmoniously. As part of this attempt to achieve harmony some of the key issues can be considered in the light of the following dichotomies:

Private	Public
Insider	Outsider
Individual	Collaborative
Formal	Informal
Formative	Summative
Qualitative	Quantitative

This list has not been drawn up in order to suggest that all the items on one side are better than those on the other side; and it should not be assumed that any evaluation programme should be composed of elements that are drawn from only one side of the list. The examples of evaluation studies quoted earlier in this chapter indicate that eclecticism marks INSET studies: evaluators draw on a number of methods to meet the particular contexts in which they are working.

In the current educational climate, where schools are increasingly seeing themselves engaged in competition for pupils and for resources, evaluators need to be particularly sensitive to the availability of their findings. Although external evaluators often seek to render schools and teachers anonymous in any written reports, there is still an awareness among LEA staff, heads of schools and teachers that any critical comments will rebound on them. External evaluators usually give close attention to the ethical contexts of their work and this permits information of a sensitive nature to be treated by them in ways that do not cause anxiety for persons whose work has been subject to evaluation. The matter of privacy is particularly significant for those evaluators who may be engaged in seeking changes in pupils' or teachers' behaviour in classrooms. One has only to think of the discussions that have taken place about the role of systematic classroom observation in teacher appraisal to appreciate the importance attached by teachers to their private classroom work. Experience suggests that the matter of privacy is central to the concerns of LEAs and staffs in schools when they consider evaluation. Stories abound of difficulties arising as a result of private evaluation information becoming available in a public way, and these stories provide the context in which INSET evaluation is currently undertaken. It is important for evaluators to be clear at the outset about the ownership of any evaluation study and the precise audience that will have access to any evaluation reports. The process of verification referred to in the meta-evaluation study earlier in this chapter is an important procedure in avoiding any misunderstandings and misinterpretations of data.

The use of external evaluators for INSET evaluation was a feature that gained prominence in TRIST. LEAs were encouraged to appoint external evaluators and funding was available through the INSET pool for LEAs to second teachers to be trained as evaluators or to engage in LEA-organized evaluation projects. The sharp reduction in teacher secondments has meant that fewer teachers are being trained for this task. Attachment of a teacher to an institution of higher education provided not only training but also a distance factor, which enabled a teacher from an LEA to be considered as an external evaluator by that LEA. Certainly, establishing an appropriate distance from the evaluation object is one of the problems of INSET evaluation, as it is of other aspects of educational evaluation. The problem lies in achieving a balance between the possession of local knowledge and understanding and the detachment of the evaluator who comes to a particular local context as a stranger who sees things from a fresh perspective. The stranger does not have to live with the products of his or her evaluation studies. If the studies are summative in character, yielding a final report for someone else to read and introduce any changes as a result of the report, then the external evaluator can close the door on the study as soon as the final line is written. For the internal evaluator such disinterested detachment is impossible. By definition the internal evaluator is a part of the context in which the subject for the evaluation is set.

One of the problems within LEAs is that at any time they may be engaged in a number of diverse projects, each of which requires an evaluation study. A single school may be visited by evaluators from different projects, each of whom may have a different perception of the role of evaluation and a different methodology. For teachers who are unfamiliar with the principles and practice of evaluation this variety can be confusing. I encountered this in an LEA that had evaluators simultaneously engaged in a primary school curriculum project, an INSET evaluation project and a TVEI evaluation project. The difficulty in understanding evaluation lay less with the teachers than with the advisory staff who were responsible for guiding the evaluators. Thus the evaluator of the primary school curriculum evaluation project was encouraged to develop a methodology that yielded quantitative data. The emphasis was to be on pupil-testing procedures and changes were to be recorded in statistical tables. The INSET evaluator was encouraged to produce qualitative data that illustrated from observation and interview findings the effectiveness of INSET provision, and to make judgements about the quality of various types of INSET provision. However, the TVEI evaluator was an advocate of value-free evaluation methods and argued that the task was to describe various aspects of TVEI in a readable way, so that teachers and others could come to their own conclusions; it was left for the readers to make any judgements which they considered necessary. Such a variety of experience is commonplace in LEAs. Some have sought to develop a unified evaluation policy in order to reduce the level of confusion, but the complicated structures of LEAs, the evaluation requirements of different bodies sponsoring projects in LEAs and the individual characteristics of evaluators make it virtually impossible to construct such policies. Similarly, while evaluators require the collaboration of the persons who are the targets of evaluation studies they often experience difficulty in collaborating with others on evaluation tasks. Evaluation in education can be a very fluid activity, even when tightly planned, and achieving a common understanding between collaborative evaluators is often difficult. Much depends on the scale of the evaluation task being undertaken, but considerations of costs alone usually mean that solitary evaluators are more commonplace than pairs or groups.

The word 'formal' is used to highlight the setting up of an evaluation project in which the target for the evaluation is carefully delineated, the aims are carefully defined, an evaluator is appointed specifically to conduct the study, the audience for the study is determined, and a formal contract including reference to payment of any fees, the timescale for the study, and the type of product, summative or formative, quantitative or qualitative, is stated. Such an arrangement differs sharply from an informal evaluation, where all these details are left unstated. Such an informal arrangement would characterize self-evaluation. Here an INSET provider or a client may consciously and deliberately engage in evaluation although there may be no formal evidence to indicate that any evaluation had taken place. Discussions held immediately after an INSET activity, in corridors, dining rooms, car parks and staff rooms, may be considered to be part of the debriefing that characterizes much informal evaluation. The encouragement of individuals to engage in informal self-evaluation is partly a recognition that formal evaluation is expensive in time and money and that there is a shortage of trained evaluators. It is also a recognition that even where LEAs or schools have evaluation expertise any formal evaluation undertaken will only touch the tip of a very large iceberg.

Reference has already been made to formative and summative methods of INSET evaluation. In the examples of evaluation studies quoted earlier in this chapter the importance of formative evaluation was obvious. Consideration of formative and summative evaluation serves to highlight the distinction between processes and products. Formative evaluation is undertaken to provide information, insights and judgements about processes as they are being developed. Formative reports may be seen as interventions in the on-going activity. For INSET this means that during an event or course an evaluator contributes interim reports to the provider and, possibly, to the clients. These reports may change the nature of the INSET provision as it develops or the next time a similar event or course is provided. Formative evaluation is also important for the development of INSET structures. An evaluator can assist in, for example, the development of school INSET co-ordinators or the evolution of teams of advisory teachers.

In all the studies quoted in this chapter the preference of the evaluators has been for qualitative methods. Given that INSET activities are principally concerned with changing teachers' behaviour and eventually with changing pupils' learning experiences in schools, it might be expected that evaluation studies would focus heavily on pre-tests of teachers and/or pupils, followed by careful monitoring of training activities and then post-testing of teachers and/or pupils. However, such a simple sequence of evaluation events is rarely, if ever, encountered.

8 Towards the future

England and Wales enter the 1990s with a radical programme of educational reform that has profound implications for the control and management of schools, the curriculum and the definition of the role of teachers. This programme has been initiated by central government, which has established a structure where decision-making is firmly located at the centre and the role of local education authorities and professionals in the schools has been sharply limited. This reform has demanded and is continuing to demand a response from teachers, who are expected to implement in a short time span the government's plans. Yet it is obvious that despite much goodwill and professional determination the changes are taking place in the context of teacher shortage and inadequate teacher preparation.

The factual background is clearly evident in the 1988 Secondary School Staffing Survey undertaken by the Department of Education and Science. In March 1988, data were gathered from a 10 per cent sample of maintained secondary schools in England. Altogether 424 schools and 17,900 teachers provided information about teachers' qualifications and deployment, the organization of the curriculum in schools and the teachers' experience of INSET. What emerges is a picture of chronic teacher shortage, especially in subjects such as mathematics, science, design and technology, modern languages and music. The figures are reinforced by the recruitment records from teacher training establishments, which demonstrate a shortfall in the number of students being trained for these and other subjects. Not only is there a difficulty of recruitment, there is also employment of non-specialist teachers in secondary schools to teach core subjects. The DES figures show that, in 1988, 27 per cent of teachers of mathematics, 31 per cent of teachers of physics, 48 per cent of teachers of craft, design and technology, 28 per cent of teachers of English and 18 per cent of teachers of French had not gained a post A-level qualification in the subjects. This hidden shortage enables schools to cope with the curriculum and, while there are many teachers who are able to teach adequate or even good lessons in their non-specialist subjects, it cannot be argued that this is a satisfactory foundation on which to build a reformed school system.

There is a strong argument for retraining the redeployed teachers in the hidden shortage area. The opportunities for such retraining have been reduced as schools and LEAs have sought to implement INSET policies that are increasingly focused on short-term 'fire fighting' measures, designed to give teachers the minimum information and skills necessary for implementing the programmes of study in the National Curriculum.

The DES Secondary School Staffing Survey (DES 1989c) findings make interesting reading for INSET specialists. One table (no. 27) gives details of INSET courses by subject and length. Of teachers attending INSET courses full-time for more than six days, the majority attended courses in education management, remedial subjects, information technology and needlecraft. The percentages were generally higher in the part-time context, with craft showing the highest figure of 16 per cent of teachers participating in INSET attending courses of more than 16 hours. In no other subject or theme did the comparable figure rise above 10 per cent.

The figures showing the venues where teachers went for INSET are illuminating. Data are provided for school subjects under six headings: the teacher's school, another school, a teachers' centre, a further or higher education college, a university, and elsewhere. By combining the figures for the first three items in this list it is possible to see the emphasis given to school-based and LEA-based INSET. For the core subjects of the National Curriculum the figures for school- and LEA-based

INSET are: mathematics 79 per cent, general science 76 per cent (separate sciences: biology 77 per cent, chemistry 89 per cent, physics 80 per cent), English 89 per cent. Not surprisingly, given the introduction of staff development days in schools, the figures for INSET in the teachers' own schools are relatively high in all cases.

It is against this backcloth that any view of the future development of INSET must be set. The whole conception of the continuing professional development of teachers, perceived as the preparation of teachers for lifelong education (Goad 1984), would appear to be a romantic one. It appears to have a rainbow's end quality – eminently attractive and desirable but unachievable. Not only does the current mode of fire fighting fly in the face of the evolving professionalism of the teacher, it is also paralleled by government initiatives, such as the articled teacher and the licensed teacher schemes, that confuse the three training stages highlighted by the James Report: initial, induction and in-service. While acknowledging that there are strong forces operating against any conception of the continuing professional development of teachers, it is important to continue to argue the case and develop the necessary infrastructure to accommodate such a conception.

There are two major themes, beyond the changes being introduced following the passing of the Education Reform Act, that will seriously affect the professionalism of teachers in England and Wales. First, economic and social forces will result in the recruitment, from a declining number of graduate students, of highly skilled manpower by the industrial and commercial sectors. It is widely assumed that in an enterprise culture teaching as a career will be unable to compete in terms of salary, conditions of service and status with industrial and commercial organizations. Secondly, the introduction in 1992 of the new European Community arrangements, which will facilitate the movement of teachers between countries, will highlight the comparability of teachers' qualifications and the variations between EC countries in teachers' salaries, conditions of service and status.

Both these themes – competition for graduates and comparability of definitions of the profession – require that close attention should be paid to the continuing professional development of teachers in England and Wales. If teaching is to attract a share of the available graduates it will need to demonstrate that a teacher can grow in the profession and that this growth will be adequately rewarded. Similarly, in the European context, teachers in England and Wales will have their attention drawn to the salary structures in those European countries that offer rewards to teachers who can demonstrate that they have improved their level of qualification.

What this points to is the need to identify a professional development ladder for teachers, which has built into it levels of award. Such a ladder should recognize formally the energy and commitment of teachers to their personal professional development. It should provide yardsticks against which teachers can measure their improving professionalism. It should also facilitate the mobility of teachers within England and Wales, as well as between EC member states, by defining qualifications that should have national and international standing.

Some of the levels of award are already clear. First, there is qualified teacher status, which is accorded to teachers who have successfully completed a period of initial teacher training. Secondly, there is the master's level, which indicates that a teacher has been able to engage in professional and/or academic study or research within an institution of higher education. Between these two levels there is currently a great variety of INSET provision, award-bearing and non-award-bearing. This provision includes enhancement of initial teacher training qualifications, and initial training and retraining in new subjects and for new knowledge and skills. Even a brief perusal of the awards available in institutions of higher education reveals a great variety of award-bearing courses, carrying titles such as Certificate in Advanced Studies in Education, Certificate of Further Professional Studies, Diploma in Advanced Studies in Education and so on. In addition, there are certificates and diplomas that are confined to particular school subjects, phases of education or educational issues. Determining the comparability of these awards and defining the appropriate level of an award are difficult tasks even for those who construct the courses. For teachers, selecting the appropriate course to follow can be equally difficult. Bringing some order into this untidy state of affairs is an essential first step in designing the professional career ladder. This task is especially important for universities and steps have been taken by the Universities Council for the Education of Teachers to clarify the position with regard to diplomas offered by university departments and schools of education.

As was described in Chapter 5, the introduction of the UCET Credit Transfer Agreement has helped universities to establish a common tariff for course units at master's level. This parallels the pattern of awards accredited by the CNAA. This, in structural terms, marks an important stage in the development of the professional career ladder. Its importance for the providers needs to be placed alongside the importance attached to it by teachers. The possibility of credit transfer is currently of interest to a small number of mobile teachers, and it is difficult to predict how quickly teachers will adjust to the possibility of following parts of an award-bearing taught course in more than one institution. In 1990 crossing the binary line is still something of a rarity, although the possibility of more such crossings would appear to be likely with the participation of seven universities (Bradford, Brunel, City, Keele, Sheffield, Warwick and Oxford's Department of External Studies) in the CNAA's Credit Transfer and Accumulation Scheme (CATS) (Yarde 1989).

A study undertaken by Triggs and Francis (1989) throws light on the value placed by persons in the education service upon advanced award-bearing courses. Evidence obtained from questionnaire returns from samples of respondents drawn from university heads of education departments, LEAs, headteachers and students attending award-bearing courses indicated that:

Awards are highly respected within the profession. And they cannot be readily replaced with other types of course recognition. For those involved *in* long term award bearing courses, the accreditation of any and every kind of in-service course in relation to a wide variety of awards, must vitiate the value of the awards themselves. For those involved *with* these courses, awards must continue to have valid currency, whatever changes need to be made to the courses that lead to them and however much circumstances in the field change.

Triggs and Francis pinpoint two issues for the future. First, they argue that the 'organisation of INSET, nationally as well as locally, needs to be seen as a whole, with each individual programme contributing to the solution of a practical issue at some level and/or contributing towards a widely recognised level of award'. Secondly, they argue for the introduction of a teachers' 'record of experience', or profile, to incorporate the in-service training experiences of teachers.

Locating INSET in the whole professional development career of the teacher, and recognizing this in a formal way, lie in these conclusions of Triggs and Francis. The conclusions fit firmly into the patterns of professional development that have been discussed by a working party meeting at regular intervals since 1988 and bringing together representatives drawn from the CNAA, UCET and SCETT (Standing Conference on Education and Teacher Training). The members of this working party have sought to define a framework that accommodates three principal levels of award – qualified teacher status, diploma and master's – and takes account of teachers' increasing professional experience within classrooms, schools and the wider education system. Central to such a framework are the increasing professional knowledge and skills of the teacher and the capacity of the teacher to engage in critical reflection on his or her own professional experience and on the system of which this experience is a part. Such a framework offers a context in which to locate current INSET provision and gives a target for future changes in provision. Current provision is largely inadequate because of its lack of a reflective emphasis. It is concerned more with a basic level of coping than with a more mature, reflective stance. As such it is episodic in character, lacking any sequential structure or provision for incremental growth. It ignores arguments for progression, balance, depth, breadth and differentiation in the continuing professional development of teachers. Equally, it ignores the needs-based model of INSET that is promulgated in LEATGS. Teachers are having their needs defined for them, not by them. These needs are rarely located in any professional development structure that has been negotiated by teachers with their employers. Such a structure should include nationally recognized levels, should enable teachers to obtain credit and awards for INSET experience, and should provide for a system of recording the credit and awards. Promotion and the payment of extra salary have not been associated with the in-service awards obtained by teachers in England and Wales. As steps are taken towards local bargaining for teachers' salaries such payment may become increasingly common.

The major trends in INSET in England and Wales reviewed in this book suggest the ways that INSET is likely to develop in the future. The following list is an attempt to draw these suggestions together.

1. Experience of TRIST, GRIST and LEATGS has stimulated teachers' expectations for INSET. The accelerating pace of educational reform will heighten these expectations but teachers will become increasingly frustrated by the lack of sufficient funding to ensure that their expectations can be matched by provision.

2. Even if sufficient funding is made available, schools will be unable to cope with the amount of teacher absence from classrooms that is a consequence of INSET provision during school time. Increasing concern is being expressed, especially in small primary schools, about the discontinuities in the experience of children resulting from teacher absence. In many parts of England and Wales supply cover for teachers is not easily obtained. Headteachers frequently complain that experienced teachers in specialized subjects are being temporarily replaced by supply teachers, who are often insufficiently trained and are little more than childminders. There is likely to be a reduction in the amount of teacher absence from school to attend INSET activities.

189

3. The shift away from award-bearing long courses provided principally by institutions of higher education is likely to continue. The later 1980s has seen the collapse of full-time secondments of teachers to attend such courses and as schools become responsible for their own staff development policies and associated budgets it is unlikely that schools will wish to second their teachers to attend full-time courses.

4. Associated with this shift is the change in the role of advisers, who will have a role that will emphasize inspection of teachers and schools. Advisers will become planners, monitors and evaluators rather than INSET providers. Their providing role will pass to advisory teachers and teacher support groups established to assist in bringing in the National Curriculum. These support staff will require special training, although the pressure and speed of change are likely to ensure that this will be inadequate.

5. Given the dependence of INSET planning and structures upon central government funding, the continuity of the annual cycle of planning and implementation of INSET will continue. The INSET agenda will focus sharply on national priorities framed by the National Curriculum and new pupil assessment arrangements. The need to establish structures to revise programmes of study, even before these programmes have been determined, is evident and this will ensure that the same patterns of priorities will continue into the next century. However, INSET planners at LEA and school levels will be unable to plan for the middle and long term with the surety of adequate funding.

6. The tension between teachers' personal professional needs and the needs of functional groups in schools, whole schools and LEAs will continue and teachers will struggle to ensure that their personal needs receive appropriate recognition.

7. The shift of INSET provision away from agencies at a distance from schools and towards advisory teachers will see a greater concentration on the individual school as the venue for INSET provision. The provision of courses is likely to become increasingly difficult. Even more attention will need to be paid to improving the effectiveness of staff development days and to introducing alternatives to courses. The increasing sophistication of training methods associated with new technologies will provide opportunities for individualization of INSET provision, enabling teachers to gain access to expertise from local, regional, national

and international sources at times and in places convenient to them. Many teachers are already familiar with the beginnings of these alternatives through their experience of the Open University and experiments with self-supported study.

8. Quality circles extending beyond individual schools into local consortia and clusters, already well established in many LEAs and especially through TVEI, will become increasingly active, not least because of their relatively low cost. These self-help and teacher support groups focus the attention of teachers on their own local problems and issues. They are responsive to local needs and are low cost operations, since they do not necessarily involve any high cost external assistance. Provided that they meet primarily outside school hours, these groups will become increasingly significant.

9. The introduction of GRIST and LEATGS has led to an increasing professionalization of INSET co-ordinators at LEA and school levels. This process is likely to continue as schools become responsible for more local management decisions. Teachers, as human capital, will need to be cared for as the teacher shortage intensifies into the 1990s. Staff development and INSET development will require more and more attention. The introduction to schools of teacher appraisal will ensure that staff development policies will need to be carefully and sensitively formulated and effectively implemented. Responsibility for this will fall on the school INSET co-ordinators, who are likely to figure prominently in senior management.

10. The evaluation role of school INSET co-ordinators and advisory teachers continues to be underplayed. INSET evaluation is a highly skilled activity requiring thorough training. Unlike TRIST, GRIST and LEATGS have not given a sufficiently high profile to evaluation, even though LEAs are encouraged in the annual INSET circulars to develop systems for evaluation. Although the future is likely to see more careful auditing and monitoring of INSET, it is unlikely that evaluation of the results of INSET through careful formal studies of changes in teachers' classroom behaviour will become commonplace.

11. The moves towards the introduction of a teacher's 'record of INSET experience' are likely to accelerate. This will be stimulated partly by the introduction of teacher appraisal schemes and partly by the introduction of such records in initial teacher training. As CATE (Council for the Accreditation of Teacher Education) criteria for

initial teacher training become more prescriptive, it becomes more likely that student teachers will leave their courses with such formal records. Should they become part of the probation procedure in schools, such records will assist in promoting the arguments for a structure for the continuing professional development of teachers. It is likely that the record of experience will come before the structure.

Bibliography

Adams, E. (ed.) (1975). *In-Service Education and Teachers' Centres*. Oxford: Pergamon Press.

Advisory Committee on the Supply and Training of Teachers (1974). *In-Service Education and Training*. London: Department of Education and Science.

Advisory Committee on the Supply and Training of Teachers (1978). *Making INSET Work*. London: Department of Education and Science.

Advisory Committee on the Supply and Education of Teachers (1984). *The In-Service Education, Training and Professional Development of School Teachers*. Report of the Teacher Training Sub-Committee. London: Department of Education and Science.

Battle, S., Davies, P., Dovaston, V., Evans, K., Lloyd, P. and Yates, J. (1988). *National Evaluation Report: An Evaluation of TRIST Management*. London: Manpower Services Commission.

Bell, G. and Rice, C. (eds) (undated). *The Role of the Staff Development Tutor*. Manchester: North West TRIST and Manpower Services Commission.

Bell, L. A. (1979). The development of an evaluation instrument for an in-service short course. *British Journal of In-Service Education*, 6 (1), 43–7.

Bell, L. A. (1980). The evaluation of an in-service course 1: the planning. *British Journal of In-Service Education*, 7 (1), 38–48.

Board of Education (1944a). *Teachers and Youth Leaders*. Report of the Committee appointed by the President of the Board of Education to consider the supply, recruitment and training of teachers and youth leaders (McNair Report). London: HMSO.

Board of Education (1944b). Circular 1652. *The Emergency Recruitment and Training of Teachers, to be operated when circumstances permit*. London: Board of Education.

Bolam, R. (1975). The management of educational change: towards a conceptual framework. In Harris, A., Lawn, M. and Prescott, W. (eds), *Curriculum Innovation*. London: Croom Helm/Open University Press.

Bolam, R. (ed.) (1982). *School-Focussed In-Service Training*. London: Heinemann Educational Books.

Brugelmann, H. (1976). *The Teachers' Centre* (SAFARI Case Studies No. 1). Norwich: Centre for Applied Research in Education. University of East Anglia.

Bunnell, S. (ed.) (1989). *Teacher Appraisal in Practice*. London: Heinemann Educational Books.

Capell, A., Mills, D. and Poster, C. (1987). *Training and Development Needs Questionnaire: Handbook for Schools*. Bristol: National Development Centre for School Management Training.

Carr, W. and Kemmis, S. (1986). *Becoming Critical: Education, Knowledge and Action Research*. Lewes: Falmer Press.

Central Advisory Council for Education (England) (1954). *Early Leaving*. London: HMSO.

Central Advisory Council for Education (England) (1959). *15 to 18* (Crowther Report). London: HMSO.

Central Advisory Council for Education (Wales) (1961). *Technical Education in Wales* (Oldfield Davies Report). London: HMSO.

Central Advisory Council (1963). *Half Our Future* (Newsom Report). London: HMSO.

Central Advisory Council (England) (1967). *Children and Their Primary Schools* (Plowden Report). London: HMSO.

Central Advisory Council for Education (Wales) (1968). *Primary Education in Wales* (Gittins Report). London: HMSO.

Chin, R. and Benne, K. D. (1969). General strategies for effecting change in human systems. In Bennis, W. G., Benne, K. D. and Chin, R. (eds), *The Planning of Change*, 2nd edn. London: Holt, Rinehart & Winston.

Committee of Inquiry appointed by the Secretary of State (1972). *Teacher Education and Training* (James Report). London: Department of Education and Science.

Committee on Higher Education (1963). *Higher Education* (Robbins Report). London: HMSO.

Cooper, C. and Sellors, W. (1977). Evaluation of an in-service course: the course tutors' views. *British Journal of In-Service Education*, 4 (1/2), 90–2.

Cronbach, L. J. (1963). Course improvement through evaluation. *Teachers College Record*, **64**, 672–83.

Cronbach, L. J., Ambron, S. R., Dornsbusch, S. M., Hess, R. D., Hornik, R. C., Phillips, D. C., Walker, D. E. and Weiner, S. S. (1980). *Toward Reform of Program Evaluation*. San Francisco: Jossey-Bass.

Department of Education and Science/Welsh Office (1972). *Education: A Framework for Expansion* (Cmnd 5174). London: HMSO.

Department of Education and Science (1977). *Educating Our Children: Four Subjects for Debate*. London: DES.

Department of Education and Science (1979). *Local Authority Arrangements for the School Curriculum*. London: HMSO.

Department of Education and Science/Welsh Office (1981). *The School Curriculum*. London: HMSO.

Department of Education and Science/Welsh Office (1983). *Teaching Quality* (Cmnd 8836). London: HMSO.

Department of Education and Science/Welsh Office (1985a). *Better Schools* (Cmnd 9469). London: HMSO.

Department of Education and Science/Welsh Office (1985b). *General Certificate of Secondary Education: A General Introduction*. London: DES.

Department of Education and Science/Welsh Office (1985c). *Proposed New Specific Grant Arrangements for the Inservice Education and Training of Teachers: A Position Paper*. London: DES.

Department of Education and Science/Welsh Office (1986). *Circular 6/86: Local Education Authority Training Grants Scheme: Financial Year 1987–88*. London: DES.

Department of Education and Science (1987). *LEA Training Grants Scheme: Monitoring and Evaluation Note by the DES*. London: DES.

Department of Education and Science (1989a). *Criteria for the Approval of Initial Teacher Training Courses*. London: DES.

Department of Education and Science (1989b). *Circular 18/89: The Education (Teachers) Regulations 1989*. London: DES.

Department of Education and Science (1989c). *From Policy to Practice*. London: DES.

Elliott-Kemp, J. and Williams, G. L. (1979). *The DION Handbook*. Sheffield: PAVIC Publications, Sheffield City Polytechnic.

Eraut, M. (1972). *In-Service Education for Innovation*. Occasional paper no. 4. London: Council for Educational Technology.

Eraut, M. (1977). Some perspectives on consultancy in in-service education. *British Journal of In-Service Education*, 4 (1/2), 95–9.

Eraut, M., Pennycuick, D. and Radnor, H. (1988). *The Local Evaluation of INSET: A Metaevaluation of TRIST*. London: Manpower Services Commission.

Gerber, R. and Lidstone, J. (eds) (1988). *Developing Skills in Geographical Education*. Brisbane: International Geographical Union with the Jacaranda Press.

Goad, L.H. (1984). *Preparing Teachers for Lifelong Education*. Oxford: Pergamon Press.

Golby, M. and Fish, M.A. (1980). School-focused INSET: clients and consultants. *British Journal of In-Service Education*, 6 (2), 83–8.

Hall, V. and Oldroyd, D. (1988). *Managing INSET in Local Education Authorities*. London: Manpower Services Commission and the National Development Centre for School Management.

Harris, D. (1987). *Openness and Closure in Distance Education*. Lewes: Falmer Press.

Henderson, E.S. (1978). *The Evaluation of In-Service Teacher Training*. London: Croom Helm.

Her Majesty's Inspectorate (HMI) (1988). *A Critique of the Implementation of the Cascade Model Used to Provide INSET for Teachers in Preparation for the Introduction of the General Certificate of Secondary Education*. London: DES.

Her Majesty's Inspectorate (HMI) (1989a). *Standards in Education 1987–1988: The Annual Report of HM Senior Chief Inspector of Schools Based on the Work of HMI in England*. London: DES.

Her Majesty's Inspectorate (HMI) (1989b). *The Implementation of the Local Education Authority Training Grants Scheme (LEATGS): Report on First Year of the Scheme 1987–1988*. London: DES.

Hodgson, V.E., Mann, S.J. and Snell, R. (eds) (1987). *Beyond Distance Teaching – Towards Open Learning*. Guildford: Society for Research into Higher Education and Open University Press.

Holly, P., James, T. and Young, J. (1987). *The Experience of TRIST: Practitioners' Views of INSET and Recommendations for the Future* (Delta Project). London: Manpower Services Commission.

Hoste, R. (1977). Evaluating an in-service course in reading. *British Journal of In-Service Education,* 4 (1/2), 84–89.

Joint Committee on Standards for Educational Evaluation (1981). *Standards for Evaluations of Educational Programs, Projects and Materials.* London: McGraw-Hill.

Joyce, B. and Showers, B (1980). Improving in-service training: the messages from research. *Educational Leadership,* 37 (5), 379–85.

Lomax, D.E. (ed.) (1973). *The Education of Teachers in Britain.* Chichester: John Wiley.

Lynch, J. and Burns, B. (1984). Non-attendance at INSET functions: some comparisons with attenders. *Journal of Education for Teaching,* 10, 164–77.

McKernan, J. (1988). The countenance of curriculum action research: traditional, collaborative, and emancipatory-critical conceptions. *Journal of Curriculum and Supervision,* 3 (3) 173–200.

McMahon, A., Bolam, R., Abbot, R. and Holly, P. (1984a and b). *Guidelines for Review and Internal Development in Schools: Primary School Handbook* and *Secondary School Handbook.* Harlow: Longman and Schools Council.

Manpower Services Commission (1985). *Arrangements for the TVEI Related In-Service Training Scheme (England and Wales)* (mimeo). London: Manpower Services Commission.

Morant, R.W. (1981). *In-Service Education within the School.* London: Allen and Unwin.

Nevo, D. (1986). The conceptualization of educational evaluation: an analytical review of the literature. In House, E.R. (ed.), *New Directions in Educational Evaluation.* Lewes: Falmer Press.

Northern Examining Association (1986). *Syllabus-specific In-Service Support towards GCSE in 1988,* Circular No. 3. Manchester: NEA.

Oldroyd, D., Smith, K. and Lee, J., (1984). *School-Based Staff Development Activities: A Handbook for Schools.* Harlow: Longman for Schools Council.

O'Sullivan, F., Jones, K. and Reid, K. (1988) *Staff Development in Secondary Schools.* London: Hodder and Stoughton.

Poster, C., Murphy, M., Cleland, I. and Hall, V. (1987). *Training and Development Needs Questionnaire – LEA Handbook.* Bristol: National Development Centre for School Management Training.

Redknap, C. (1977). *Focus on Teachers' Centres.* Windsor: NFER-Nelson.

Robinson, N. and Thompson, J. (1987). *Methods of Assessing INSET Needs.* Calderdale Metropolitan Borough Council.

Robson, C., Sebba, J., Mittler, P. and Davies, G., (1988). *In-Service Training and Special Educational Needs: Running Short, School-Focused Courses.* Manchester: Manchester University Press.

Rudd, W.G.A. (1972). Local curriculum development. In Lomax, D. E. (ed.), *The Education of Teachers in Britain.* Chichester: John Wiley, pp. 321–31.

Rudduck, J. (1981). *Making the Most of the Short In-Service Course.* Schools Council Working Paper 71. London: Methuen Educational.

Sadler, D.R. (1984). Follow-up evaluation of an in-service programme based on action research: some methodological issues. *Journal of Education for Teaching,* **10** (3), 209–18.

Schools Council (1967). *Curriculum Development: Teachers' Groups and Centres,* Schools Council Working Paper 10. London: HMSO.

Sharp, P.R (1987). *The Creation of the Local Authority Sector of Higher Education.* Lewes: Falmer Press.

Smith, P. and Kelly, M. (eds) (1987). *Distance Education and the Mainstream.* London: Croom Helm.

Thornbury, R.E. (ed.) (1973). *Teachers' Centres.* London: Darton, Longman & Todd.

Thorpe, M. (1988). *Evaluating Open and Distance Learning.* Harlow: Longman.

Triggs, E. and Francis, H. (1989). *The Value to Education of Long (Award Bearing) Courses for Serving Teachers.* London: University of London Institute of Education.

TRIST (TVEI Related In-Service Training for Teachers) (1987). *Directory of TRIST Practice.* London: Manpower Services Commission.

Turner, J.D. (1973). The area training organization. In Lomax, D.E. (ed.), *The Education of Teachers in Britain.* Chichester: John Wiley, pp. 149–74.

Universities Council for the Education of Teachers (1985). *Developing the Model: An Elaborated Response to the DES Position Paper: Proposed New Specific Grant Arrangements for the Inservice Education and Training of Teachers.* London: UCET.

Weindling, D., Reid, M.I. and Davis, P. (1983). *Teachers' Centres: A Focus for In-Service Education?* Schools Council Working Paper 74. London: Methuen Educational.

Williams, M. (1987). *Credit Transfer: In-Course Credit Recognition.* Consortium of Advanced Continuing Education and Training of the Universities of Manchester and Salford, UMIST, the Manchester Business School and Manchester Polytechnic.

Williams, M. (1988). Continuing education of geography teachers. In Gerber, R. and Lidstone, J. (eds), *Developing Skills in Geographical Education.* Brisbane: International Geographical Union with the Jacaranda Press, pp. 231–43.

Williams, M. and England, J. (1986). *Alternatives to Courses.* Manchester: TRIST North West and Manpower Services Commission.

Williams, M. and England, J. (1987). *Inter-LEA Collaboration.* TRIST paper of National Interest. London: Manpower Services Commission.

Williams, M. and England, J. (1988). The role of a TRIST consultant as a change agent. *School Organization,* 8 (1), 39–44.

Williams, M., Biilmann, O. and Gerber, R. (eds) (1988). *Towards Models for the Continuing Education of Geography Teachers.* Brisbane: Education Commission of the International Geographical Union.

Yarde, R. (1989). Seven joint credit transfer schemes. *Times Higher Education Supplement,* No. 890, 24 November, p. 5.

Name Index

Subject Index